Problem Solving and the FAE

2nd Edition

Derry Cotter

Published by
Chartered Accountants Ireland
Chartered Accountants House
47 – 49 Pearse Street
Dublin 2

www.charteredaccountants.ie

This publication is designed to provide accurate and authoritative information in regard to the subject matter covered. It is provided on the understanding that the Institute of Chartered Accountants in Ireland is not engaged in rendering professional services. The Institute of Chartered Accountants in Ireland disclaims all liability for any reliance placed on the information contained within this publication and recommends that if professional advice or other expert assistance is required, the services of a competent professional should be sought.

ISBN: 978-1-910374-31-3

Typeset by Datapage
Printed by Turner's Printing Company, Longford, Ireland

This book is dedicated to my sister Mary

To FAE students – may you find a solution to every problem

→ COLD! Bring extra / comfortable layers!!! Wear quiet shoes!

→ SLEEP - go to bed early night before!

→ PACK SUITCASE - a few days before & relax!

→ Cereal bars & gluten free crackers. 2x bottles of water.

→ Bring sticky tabs into exams - (for plans on back pages)

| TIMING | Big issue is running out of time!
         Need to practice, practice, practice cases!

1. who you are
2. indicators - identify & list (- quick read)
3. Organise the info (- focused read)
4. BIG PICTURE - type of business
   (take a step back) - industry / risk factors
                       - ownership structure etc.
5. PLANNING
   Adopt a closed book mindset
   Focus on the specifics of the case -
      ie. the situation, the client, the industry
   Every paragraph should refer to the case @
   danger of a generic answer.

Give pros & cons!

● ADD DEPTH ① Start to finish
             ② Different perspectives
             ③ Link indicators

● BE CONSISTENT computations → Analysis → Advice

● EXECUTIVE SUMMARY

DON'T SIT ON THE FENCE!

CONTENTS

Introduction

Most of us have difficulty recalling our first exposure to tasks that involved problem solving. This is because our first experience of problem solving was as babies, when we learned to insert plastic or wooden pieces into different shaped openings. I have a vivid memory of my son, at age three, identifying a momentous problem on our return home from a family outing.

"How did you get the house in through the gate?" he asked, sizing up the difficulty of the problem as he saw it. The question prompted his parents to quickly acquire a supply of Lego as a problem-solving tool. It must have worked, because he never asked the question again!

Children's stories are a favourite source of problems. Take the prince, in Cinderella, who must locate his bride-to-be, she having fled at midnight from the ball. Using the slipper left behind during her hasty departure, he has his servants embark on a tour of the kingdom to find the girl of his dreams. Thus does the prince display the skill of delegation – well, he would hardly have traipsed around the kingdom himself, now would he? As a prince, he also had the foresight to know that the slipper would fit only one girl, a fact that lesser mortals such as myself would have failed to realise.

Goldilocks was another well-known problem solver. Finding daddy bear's chair to be too hard, she tried mammy bear's chair and, predictably, it was too soft. Undeterred, Goldilocks found baby bear's chair to be exactly what she wanted. Using the same technique, she also found baby bear's bed and bowl of porridge to be most to her liking.

As adults our education in problem solving continued with super sleuth, Sherlock Holmes, another problem-solving master. Dismissing the observations of his sidekick, Dr Watson, Holmes invariably solved the most baffling of mysteries. Agatha Christie gave us Miss Marple and Hercule Poirot, and we have often marvelled at the problem-solving skills of Inspector Morse, John Rebus, Kojak and the unassuming Lieutenant Columbo.

The master playwright, Shakespeare, was no slouch when it came to problem solving and, in *Hamlet,* the bard demonstrates the power of a play within a play. Suspecting that his uncle is responsible for his father's murder, Hamlet engages a travelling troupe of actors to re-enact the crime. As planned, his uncle's innocence is duly blown, his demeanour betraying a conscience racked by guilt.

In like fashion, Chartered Accountants Ireland's Final Admitting Exam (the 'FAE') presents aspiring Chartered Accountants with a problem within a problem. The ultimate challenge or problem is how to pass the FAE and, to succeed, candidates must solve a selection of carefully chosen problems posed by FAE examiners. The challenge for the examiner is to establish which students achieve competence in the FAE. To achieve **competence** you must satisfy two fundamental criteria as outlined in **Figure 1**.

FIGURE 1: ACHIEVING COMPETENCE IN THE **FAE**

Mastery of Business Knowledge

Members of a professional body are assumed to be proficient in their chosen area of expertise. Thus, medical practitioners should have a detailed knowledge of the human body and of illnesses that can affect it. Lawyers are expected to be familiar with legal principles and with relevant case law. Engineers are experts in assessing structural issues relating to buildings.

Similarly, a Chartered Accountant is **expected to have a sound understanding of how business works**. It is for this reason that the FAE evaluates students across a broad spectrum of subject areas. A successful FAE student will have a skill set which is akin to that of a general medical practitioner. He/she will possess the knowledge to assist clients with issues involving areas as diverse as audit and assurance, business leadership, corporate and individual tax planning, finance, financial accounting and reporting, and management accounting.

A general practitioner can, of course, choose to specialise in areas such as paediatrics, surgery, geriatrics or palliative care. This type of specialist knowledge is also expected of an aspiring Chartered Accountant. Thus, in addition to proving proficiency in general business matters, an FAE student must demonstrate **detailed knowledge of a chosen elective**. Currently, there are three electives to choose from: Advanced Auditing and Assurance, Advanced Performance Management and Advanced Taxation.

From a problem-solving perspective, therefore, the task of an FAE student is similar to that facing a contestant in the hit quiz show, *Mastermind*. Here, each contestant is posed questions on his/her chosen specialist subject, followed by a series of general knowledge questions.

Acquiring an advanced level of technical knowledge is therefore of critical importance for the FAE student. Thus, it is essential to fully **understand** the technical content of areas such as IFRSs, auditing standards, tax planning options, etc. The more that you know and understand about areas such as these, the more your ability to perform in the FAE will be enhanced. Although the FAE is examined on an open book basis, it will not be feasible to acquire this knowledge during the examination. You just won't have the time to locate material and go through it.

So, throughout the FAE Course Programme, invest as much time as possible in developing your technical knowledge. In this context, the **single-discipline lectures** are a key element in ensuring that your technical knowledge is at a sufficiently advanced level in individual subject disciplines. *Note:* The FAE Competency Statement, which is published online annually, is the Institute's syllabus and a very important point of reference for students.

It is also essential to stress that knowledge entails understanding. Learning by rote is not a productive activity and, in an open book examination, it will be of little or no benefit. So, try to gain an understanding of each area that you study. This is a prerequisite for effective problem solving.

Application of Knowledge

Applying one's knowledge in a relevant way is the single most important FAE skill. To achieve competence, it is essential to address the specifics of each FAE case. Should a patient present with a severe stomach pain, for example, there is little point in a medical practitioner treating other ailments such as a sprained ankle or a sore ear. The urgency of the matter demands an immediate investigation of the patient's acute stomach symptoms. The cause of the pain must be identified and treatment administered without delay.

Similarly, when an FAE student is asked to solve a business problem, **he must be completely focused on the issue at hand**. For example, a business may be in danger of becoming insolvent due to having to service an unaffordable level of debt repayments. There is little point in suggesting that the business should improve its working capital management or that it should curtail its dividend payments. Both are laudable suggestions, but they fail to address the entity's imminent bankruptcy. **What is needed is for the business to reschedule its repayments by extending the term of its loans**. Refinancing itself in this way reduces its short-term commitments, thus providing the business with an opportunity to restore its financial health. Supplementary measures, such as improved working capital management and a suspension of dividend payments may then be proposed as additional coping mechanisms.

It should be remembered that, in an open book format, an Examiner will not reward a student for regurgitating material from readily accessible sources. General points relating to achieving improved liquidity are of little value when a firm's debt burden is about to render it bankrupt. **Instead, a competent student will address the fundamental problem of the entity's debt commitments, and suggest how these could be refinanced**.

Summary

Demonstrating competence is the core requirement for success in the FAE. This requires that successful candidates show themselves to be effective problem solvers. Armed with the requisite level of knowledge, a professional has the potential to achieve competence in his/her chosen field. Ultimately, however, the realisation of this potential requires that **knowledge is skilfully applied to identify specific solutions for specific problems**.

Acknowledgements

I wish to thank Ronan O'Loughlin for recommending that this book be published, and Michael Diviney for commissioning it. I also wish to acknowledge the constructive advice and suggestions provided by Joanne Powell.

Thanks too to Becky McIndoe and the editing and design team at Chartered Accountants Ireland for their invaluable assistance.

I am also indebted to my family for their ongoing support and encouragement.

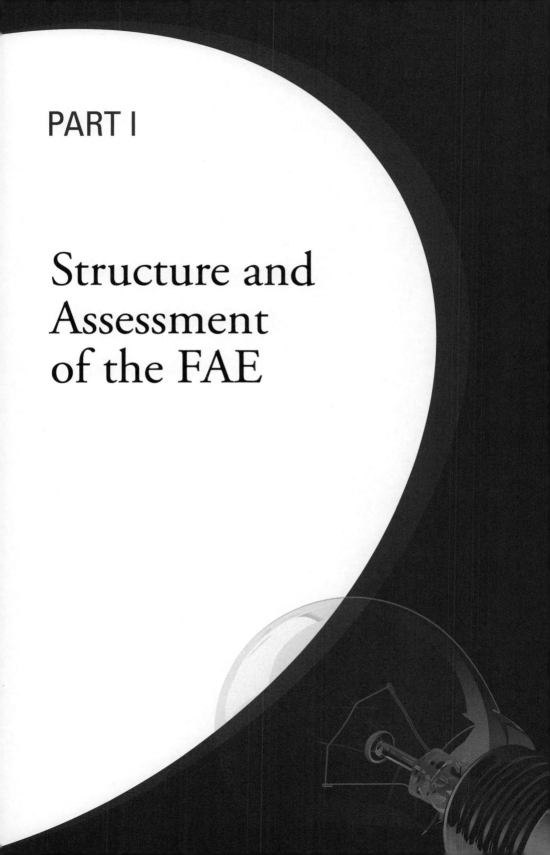

PART I

Structure and Assessment of the FAE

Chapter 1. Structure of the FAE

The FAE consists of two components:

1. FAE Core:
   - Core Comprehensive (Paper 1)
   - Core Simulations (Paper 2)
   - Interim assessment – Advanced Application of Financial Reporting Principles (AAFRP)

   and

2. FAE Elective:
   - Interim assessment
   - Paper 3 – at the end of the year

The content of each of these areas is now outlined in detail.

A. FAE Core

Paper 1 – FAE Core Comprehensive

Paper 1 consists of a single 4-hour case study (plus 30 minutes reading time), which requires students to have an understanding of a broad spectrum of business modules. The specific modules are subject to change and students should refer to the Competency Statement for their given year, which can be accessed at www.charteredaccountants.ie. Currently, there are six business modules[1]:

1. Auditing and Assurance
2. Business Leadership
3. Corporation and Individual Tax Planning
4. Finance
5. Financial Accounting and Reporting
6. Management Accounting.

Students should refer to the FAE competency statement for the weighting of these subject areas.

The paper contains approximately **seven to nine primary indicators**, which equates to **seven to nine individual issues that must be addressed in the case study**. For example, a candidate may identify a firm's choice of transfer pricing methods as an important issue. This would constitute one primary indicator.

---

[1] These six modules are colloquially known as the 'Super Six', a term coined by FAE lecturer, Paul Monahan.

Paper 2 – FAE Core Simulations

This paper consists of two shorter case studies, each of which is called a 'simulation'. The total time allowed is 4 hours (plus 30 minutes reading time). These case studies also require an understanding of all of the business modules outlined above (again referring to the relevant Competency Statement for any given year). Each simulation contains approximately three to five primary indicators.

In total, FAE Core Papers 1 and 2 contain approximately 15–19 primary indicators. This requires a candidate to identify 15–19 issues across all the business modules and over the two case study papers that comprise the FAE Core end-of-year examination.

Interim Assessment – AAFRP

Advanced Application of Financial Reporting Principles (AAFRP) assesses a candidate's technical ability, judgement and decision-making abilities in double-entry accounting, presentation of financial information and financial reporting disclosure. A candidate's result in the AAFRP assessment **counts as one primary indicator** in the Financial Accounting and Reporting module.

B. FAE Elective

All candidates must complete one FAE Elective module. Currently, candidates can choose from the following options:
■ Advanced Auditing and Assurance
■ Advanced Performance Management
■ Advanced Taxation (NI or ROI variant).

Again, students should refer to the Competency Statement for the module options available to them in any given year.

A candidate's chosen elective is examined by:
■ an interim assessment worth one primary indicator, and
■ Paper 3, a 4-hour (plus 30 minutes reading time) end-of-year examination. This paper comprises two case studies, each containing three to five primary indicators.

Summary

The FAE consists of the FAE Core and the FAE Elective.

FAE Core comprises Core Comprehensive (Paper 1) and Core Simulations (Paper 2), both of which require coverage of all of the business modules as outlined in the Competency Statement. The AAFRP, which is an interim assessment on double entry, is also part of FAE Core.

FAE Elective requires candidates to choose one subject area as outlined in the Competency Statement. The FAE Elective is examined by an interim assessment and Paper 3 of the end-of-year examinations.

Chapter 2. Assessment of the FAE

Introduction

Each FAE case study contains a number of primary indicators (i.e. issues). Each primary indicator is separately assessed on a scale that goes from 'Not Addressed' to 'Highly Competent'. For each of the three FAE papers, these 'indicator competency scores' are collected together. An adjudication is then made as to whether a candidate has satisfied the competence requirements set by the FAE Board.

End-of-Year Papers

The end-of-year papers comprise:
- Core Comprehensive (one case study);
- Core Simulations (two case studies); and
- Elective (two case studies).

As explained in **Chapter 1** a candidate is required to address a number of primary indicators (i.e. issues) in each FAE case. For each primary indicator, the candidate's answer is rated on a scale as outlined in **Figure 2.1**.

FIGURE 2.1: ASSESSMENT SCALE FOR PRIMARY INDICATORS

Not Addressed	The candidate does not address this primary indicator; no attempt made.
Nominal Competence	Candidate makes an attempt, but little of reasonable value written.
Basic Competence	Some value in response but not assessed as 'Competent', either due to absence of significant point(s) or level of depth of discussion.
Competent	Response demonstrates a level of depth and adequate appreciation of key points. A clear decision or recommendation is made where appropriate.
Highly Competent	The '90%' solution: good depth and grasp of issues (including peripheral ones). Response adds further value, etc.

Consider a fairground stall where two tin cans are positioned slightly apart and a third one placed on top straddling both of its supporters. You are standing about eight feet away and the assistant hands you three balls. The challenge is to knock all of the cans from the table on which they are resting.

The first ball slips from your grasp and falls harmlessly to the ground, i.e. 'Not Addressed'. With the second, you use as much force as you can muster but you miss the target by a long way, i.e. 'Nominal Competence'. Your third throw knocks the top can from its perch, leaving the other two standing, i.e. 'Basic Competence'.

You decide to try again, so the assistant restores the cans to their original position and hands you another three balls. This time you concentrate more on accuracy than power and you again manage to displace the top can, i.e. 'Basic Competence'. Your second ball moves the remaining two cans closer to the edge of the table, again 'Basic Competence', and you punch the air as your third sends them toppling to the ground, i.e. 'Competent'. You receive a token from the assistant, and he points to a row of small teddy bears on the shelf behind him.

Putting the token in your pocket you decide to go for one of the prizes on the second row of the shelf. At your next attempt you knock down another set of cans with your first ball. Handing over both tokens you choose a yellow teddy bear from the upper shelf. On this occasion you have completed the task with greater accuracy and skill, you are 'Highly Competent'.

Interim Assessments

AAFRP is assessed using a traditional marking scheme approach. Each question is marked according to the level of accuracy shown by the candidate. Ultimately, each candidate's score is translated to an overall competency ranking as outlined in **Figure 2.1** above.

There is also an elective interim assessment, which will be assessed on the basis of sufficiency.

Adjudication of FAE Scripts[*]

A. FAE Core

For FAE Core, adjudication takes place at three levels: sufficiency, depth and breadth. For the Core Comprehensive case and the three Core Simulation cases, **a successful candidate must obtain a 'pass' in each of the three levels**. An overall result for each of the three levels is obtained for FAE Core. The requirement is represented in **Figure 2.2**.

FIGURE 2.2: ACHIEVING COMPETENCE IN FAE CORE

Sufficiency   This is Level 1. To pass this level, a candidate must demonstrate sufficient overall competence. A candidate is allocated a value for each indicator as follows:

- two points are obtained each time 'Basic Competence' is achieved;
- four points are obtained each time 'Competent' or 'Highly Competent' is achieved.

In order to achieve 'Sufficiency', candidates must typically attain at least 50% of the available credits (i.e. 50% of four points multiplied by the total number of indicators). A candidate can achieve the required value using any combination of the business modules that comprise the 'Super Six'.

[handwritten margin note: eg 15 indicators × 4 points = 60 points must get 30 points across board]

---

[*] Specific guidance is provided in the *FAE Marking and Adjudication Parameters: Guidance for Candidates* issued by the FAE Examinations Board for the academic year.

Depth   This is Level 2. To pass this level, a candidate must demonstrate depth in each of Business Leadership and Financial Accounting and Reporting. A candidate is allocated a value for each indicator as follows:

■ four points are obtained each time 'Competent' or 'Highly Competent' is achieved.

A candidate must achieve 'Competent' or 'Highly Competent' on 50% or more of the available indicators in both Business Leadership **and** Financial Accounting and Reporting in order to pass this level.

Competent or HC in >50% of BL & FR indicators.

Breadth   This is Level 3. To pass this level, a candidate must demonstrate breadth in each of Audit, Tax, Finance and Management Accounting.

A candidate is allocated a value for each indicator as follows:

■ two points are obtained each time 'Basic Competence' or higher is achieved.

A candidate must achieve 'Basic Competence' or higher, on 50% or more of the available indicators in **each** of the four areas listed above in order to pass this level.

To understand the above scoring system, let's return to the fairground where the owners have offered a special entrance pass to visitors who achieve competence in six games. To obtain the pass, you are presented with three challenges, each of which you must master.

Challenge 1 (sufficiency)   In addition to the cans task, which we have already discussed, the owners have identified five other games. These are the donkey derby, a rings challenge, a darts accuracy test, landing balls in a milk urn, and the rifle range. To 'pass' challenge 1, you must reach an overall target score, by adding together your scores across all games. You will obtain two points each time you are judged to achieve 'Basic Competence' in any of the games, and four points when you are deemed 'Competent' or 'Highly Competent'.

You must achieve at least fifty per cent of the maximum number of points available (i.e. you must score 50% × 4 × total number of indicators in FAE Core).

Challenge 2 (depth)   The fairground owners have put a special emphasis on the donkey derby and the rifle range tests. To 'pass' this challenge, you must achieve a target score in **both** of these games. You will obtain four points each time that you are deemed 'Competent' or 'Highly Competent' in the donkey derby and the rifle range. In each of these two games you must obtain four points in at least half of the available indicators. (For example, in the event that there were five donkey derby games you would have to achieve four points in at least three of the five.)

Challenge 3 (breadth)   The fairground owners also want to ensure that you do not obtain the entrance pass if you lack competence in **any** of the games. So they also require you to achieve a target score in the cans' test, the rings challenge, the darts accuracy test and landing balls in the milk urn. Each time that you achieve 'Basic Competence' or higher, you will obtain a score of two points. For **each** of the four games you must obtain at least two points in half of the available tests. (For example, if there were three darts accuracy tests you would have to achieve two points (or more) in at least two of the three tests.)

So, to pass the three challenges, you need to show:
- your overall games competence throughout the fairground;
- a high level of skill in the donkey derby and the rifle range; and
- proficiency at each of the other four games, albeit at a lower level of competence.

Satisfy these requirements and you will obtain the free entrance pass to the fairground.

B. FAE Elective

As outlined in **Chapter 1**, the FAE Elective contains an interim assessment and an end-of-year assessment. The interim assessment is an open-book scenario-based paper and the end-of-year paper comprises three case studies, each of which contains three to five primary indicators/issues.

For FAE Elective, adjudication takes place only at the level of Sufficiency.

A candidate is allocated a value/score for each indicator as follows:
- two points are obtained each time 'Basic Competence' is achieved; and
- four points are obtained each time 'Competent' or 'Highly Competent' is achieved.

To pass the FAE Elective a candidate must attain 50% of the available points (i.e. 50% of four multiplied by the total number of indicators).

C. Overall FAE Result

Candidates who pass both FAE Core and FAE Elective, either in the current exam session or when combined with a previous exam session (in accordance with FAE regulations), are awarded an overall 'pass'.[2]

Candidates who pass either FAE Core or FAE Elective may be awarded an overall 'credit', subject to FAE regulations. In this event, the area in which a credit is **not** obtained will have to be repeated by the candidate.

Candidates who fail both FAE Core **and** FAE Elective are awarded an overall 'fail'.

Summary

To pass the FAE a candidate must satisfy the requirements of the FAE Board for both FAE Core and Elective elements.

---

[2] Source: FAE Board Report 2014.

The overall assessment system is summarised in **Figure 2.3**.

FIGURE 2.3: FAE – OVERALL ASSESSMENT

	Modules	Number of Primary Indicators	Adjudication Level
1. FAE Core			
Comprehensive	Super Six	7–9	Sufficiency, Depth and Breadth
Simulations	Super Six Super Six	Case 1: 3–5 Case 2: 3–5	
Interim Assessment (AAFRP)	Financial Accounting and Reporting	1	
2. FAE			
End of year examination	Advanced Auditing, Taxation or Performance Management	Case 1: 3–5 Case 2: 3–5	Sufficiency
Interim Assessment	As outlined in the Competency Statement	1	Sufficiency

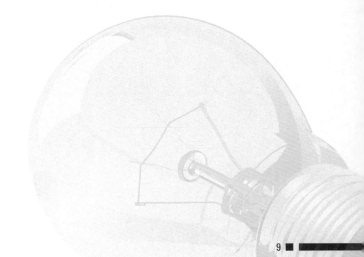

PART II

Laying the Foundations

Chapter 3. Maximise your Brain Power

The famous author, Norman Vincent Peale,[3] noted a sign at a petrol station he once visited:

"A Clean Engine Always Delivers Power."

This is a statement that we would do well to reflect on. Effective problem solving requires our brain to be working at maximum efficiency. Carefully maintained and properly nurtured, it can equally be claimed that "A Focused Brain Always Delivers Power."

We are used to looking after our physical wellbeing and that of the things we own. Dental check-ups are a normal part of life, as is the taking of medicines to treat common infections. Our cars get a regular NCT or MOT test to ensure that they are safe and running efficiently. Burglar alarms are routinely serviced, and smoke alarms are tested periodically to check if they are in proper working order.

Strangely, although our brain is constantly called upon to solve a myriad of problems, we spend little if any time in maintaining its level of efficiency. In fact, our brain is arguably the most ill-treated part of our body. Often forced to work long hours in unpleasant conditions, it is regularly deprived of the sleep that is essential for its regeneration and recovery. Eventually our thought processes become muddled and our decision-making less efficient – and we wonder why.

Clearly we are not good at providing the care and attention that our brain needs in order to operate efficiently. Mostly we do not notice our under-performance, because our lives tend to involve relatively mundane choices. Whether to walk or take the bus, for example, is normally not a difficult decision. In making such a judgement call, the weather, our desire for exercise and the amount of available time are likely to be factors we would consider.

For professional students, however, the challenges are far more intellectually demanding. In examinations the decision-making criteria are rarely routine. This is particularly true at FAE level, where critical thinking and the ability to exercise judgement are of paramount importance. Problem solving at this level requires one's brain to be functioning at a level of efficiency rarely demanded in everyday life. This is illustrated in **Figure 3.1**.

This chapter focuses on the attributes necessary for one's brain to excel in problem solving. If you are to maximise

FIGURE 3.1: DECISION-MAKING IN THE FAE

---

[3] Peale, N.V. (1974), *You Can if You Think You Can,* Simon & Schuster, New York.

your brain's potential, then concentration is a key factor. Simulating exam-type problems is also an important part of your preparation. Research shows that the brain works most efficiently when it is exposed to a type of problem that it has already solved previously. Attitude is also a factor, and problem solving improves when positive thinking becomes a basic part of one's mindset. Finally, almost anything is possible with perseverance.

These factors are summarised in **Figure 3.2** and the remainder of this chapter examines them in more detail.

FIGURE 3.2: MAXIMISING YOUR BRAIN POWER

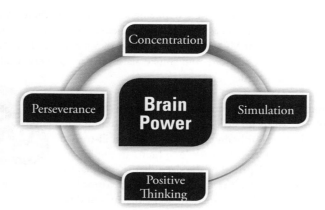

Concentration

When we are 'in the zone', problem solving is easy. Sometimes our brains process information in a way that allows us to identify convincing solutions to complex issues. You can almost hear your brain whirring as it goes about its business and, at times like this, concentration is total. So, what do we need to do to replicate this level of performance on a consistent basis?

Eliminate Interruptions

Research has found that e-mail, mobile phones and Internet usage have an adverse effect on our ability to concentrate. Picture the scene when you are presented with a problem you must solve. As you consider its intricacies, your mobile phone beeps and you divert your attention to answer a friend's text message. A minute later, the screen on your laptop flashes, and you open an e-mail recommending yet another special offer.

This type of repetitive intrusion significantly affects your capacity for problem solving. You are unable to focus sufficiently to absorb a problem's complexities or to formulate potential solutions. Griffey[4] reports the results of a Hewlett-Packard study in which "…62% of adults were addicted to their e-mail to the point where they were checking messages during meetings, after working hours and on holiday". She also refers to the contention of

---

[4] Griffey, H. (2010), *The Art of Concentration*, Rodale, London.

Stafford and Webb[5] that e-mail users are subject to the same learning mechanisms that drive gambling addicts:

> "Rather than reward an action every time it is performed, you reward it sometimes, but not in a predictable way. So with e-mail, usually when I check it there is nothing interesting, but every so often there is something wonderful – an invite out or maybe some juicy gossip – and I get a reward."

Text messages work in a similarly addictive fashion, constantly demanding our attention while adding little of consequence to our lives. So, in order to enable your brain to focus on the task at hand, distance yourself from needless distractions for the duration of your study session. Incidentally, as I write this paragraph I have had to turn off my e-mail to avoid the regular flashes signalling the arrival of new messages.

Relaxation

It is normal to feel stressed when an urgent matter puts you under pressure. Our bodies are programmed to cope with moments like this, and a rush of adrenalin will enable us to deal with the matter. Indeed, the 'fight or flight' type scenario, regularly faced by our cave-dwelling ancestors, continues to confront us from time to time. If anxiety is ongoing, however, it can severely undermine our capacity for problem solving. The brain works best when it is free from external pressures, allowing it to focus completely on the task at hand.

Thus, if you feel under stress for a sustained period of time, you should address the issue. Getting regular physical exercise is important to achieve an overall balance in our lives, and it helps to defuse any stress that has built up in our bodies and minds. Exercise can take the form of jogging or a brisk walk, a swim, a session in the gym or something more competitive for those who are so inclined.

Meditation is also a very effective way of cultivating a relaxed state of mind and sharpening one's intellect. Indeed, the story is told that the Dalai Lama, when informed that he would be extremely busy on a forthcoming tour, was heard to remark that he would have to "meditate even more". Basic meditation (or mindfulness as it is sometimes called) requires that one sit comfortably, eyes closed, and silently recite a mantra, such as a word like *shareem* which has no obvious meaning. Soon, your breathing will become deeper and you will find yourself entering a more relaxed state. Occasionally you will even find yourself falling asleep. A meditation session should typically last about 15–20 minutes and, practised regularly, will greatly improve your concentration and problem-solving abilities.

You should seek medical advice if you find that your stress levels are not reduced by using relaxation techniques or by taking regular exercise.

Sleep

A good night's sleep is a prerequisite for effective problem solving. Tiredness seriously reduces our ability to concentrate; it is often more productive to spend less time studying, enabling you to maintain maximum focus on what you are learning. This is particularly true of an open-book examination, like the FAE, where understanding and application are two of the key objectives.

---

[5] Stafford, T. & Webb, M. (2004), *Mind Hacks: Tips and Tricks for Using Your Brain*, O'Reilly Media Inc.

Diet

In her excellent book, *The Art of Concentration*, Harriet Griffey[6] deals comprehensively with the connection between diet and brain performance. She outlines how the brain's primary source of energy is glucose, which is derived from carbohydrates digested by the body. Fluctuating glucose levels reduce the brain's ability to work efficiently; and it performs best with a well-regulated supply, which is provided by eating at consistent intervals.

Some foods have a longer digestive period and release glucose more slowly over a sustained period. These are referred to as complex carbohydrates, and they include wholegrain cereals, vegetables, wholemeal pasta, beans and oats. On the other hand, simple carbohydrates, such as sugar, are digested very quickly, leading to peaks and troughs in the supply of glucose to the brain.

Protein intake is also important as it stabilises blood sugar levels and provides amino acids to our brain cells, enabling us to think more clearly. Sources of protein include meat, seafood, eggs, milk, cheese, yoghurt and beans.

Omega 3 fatty acids have also been proven to have a positive effect on brain function. The primary source is oily fish, such as mackerel, herrings, wild salmon and tuna. A fish oil supplement of Omega 3 could also be considered.

Coffee is another matter. I like coffee, and I particularly like cappuccino, which features the letters of my old alma mater, UCC. Coffee, however, contains caffeine, a stimulant that boosts the production of cortisone and adrenaline. As the brain works best when in a calm state, you should not drink coffee to excess. That's not to say, however, that you shouldn't enjoy the occasional cup of your favourite coffee bean!

Griffey maintains that there are three basic principles regarding food:
■ freshness;
■ diversity; and
■ balance.

So, for efficient brain activity you should have a well-balanced diet, rely less on products that are high in sugar, and eat fresh food as much as possible.

Frequent Study Breaks

Research has shown that the material you study at the beginning and end of a session is what you will remember best. Therefore, a study session of about 45 minutes may be optimal. You should then take a short break before starting back.

Simulation

It takes time for one's brain to adapt to a new situation. When learning to drive, for example, manoeuvres such as reversing or starting on a hill can be challenging. With practice, however,

---

[6] Griffey, H. (2010), *op. cit.*, above n.4.

we learn the skills necessary to perform these tasks with minimum difficulty. This is because our brain is at its most efficient when handling problems which it has faced many times before. Repetition reduces the level of difficulty.

In the FAE, mastering the case study technique is a skill that is best acquired throughout your FAE year and into your study leave. Gradually, as your brain adapts to the challenge, you will find yourself completing cases more skilfully and in less time.

It is critical that you spend time working on case studies as this will develop the problem-solving skills that you need in the FAE. On any one day only a very small percentage of what you study is likely to be examined. By attempting case studies, however, you are ensuring that your problem-solving skills become more routine and therefore more efficient.

The importance of practice and experience is evident from the comments of South African rugby player, B.J. Botha:[7]

> "With a little bit of experience … you're more relaxed until you hit the field. At that stage something takes over that you can't explain. You're in your own little world and you can't even hear the crowd … When I was younger you got on the field and you were buzzing. It lasts 10 minutes and then it's over. To work yourself through a game … you need concentration. You can't concentrate when you're in that mental state that you're hyped up and ready to run through a brick wall."

Clearly, concentration improves with practice. That is, as long as you are practising in the right way.

A broad range of practice case material is available to FAE students in any given year. As suggested above, FAE students should work through the relevant case material as a means of acquiring the skills expected of a qualifying Chartered Accountant. This method of study will provide far greater benefits than merely reading suggested solutions.

---

[7] Botha, B.J., *The Sunday Times*, 8 January 2012.

Positive Thinking

You Can if You Think You Can is the title of Norman Vincent Peale's[8] best-selling book from the 1970s. Peale explains how a positive attitude significantly increases your chances of success, and how motivational psychology is now employed in most walks of life. Salesmen are taught to believe that the word 'no' simply means that a customer has not yet said 'yes'. Positive thinking is now considered to be a key ingredient of sporting success. Professional golfers, for example, visualise the flight of each shot before they hit it. In rugby, place-kickers imagine the ball going straight between the posts each and every time.

Research has shown that the brain performs best when you have confidence in your ability to solve problems. So back yourself, and believe that you can do it.

As Henry Ford famously quipped, "Whether you think you can or you can't – you're right." So, visualise your success in the FAE examination. Keep this picture in your head at all times and it will help you to stay focused and meet your targets.

Perseverance

> "Genius is one per cent inspiration and ninety-nine per cent perspiration. Accordingly a genius is often merely a talented person who has done all of his or her homework."
>
> Thomas Edison

Perseverance and commitment are essential if you are to be successful in the FAE. You must recognise, however, that almost everything in life is habit forming. Your brain will perform at its best when its problem-solving capabilities are regularly challenged. Remember that it's more productive to study consistently on most days than to 'cram' for many hours every once in a while. This is particularly true of the FAE, where the case study technique is best acquired over time rather than by short periods of cramming.

The nineteenth century politician and writer, Benjamin Disraeli, emphasised the importance of perseverance when he said, "The secret of success is constancy of purpose."

So, commit yourself to the FAE. **Develop a regular study pattern**. Be patient as you learn the skills of problem solving across the range of FAE business disciplines. Most of all – **persevere!**

Summary

Most of us take the time to give regular checks to our cars and other possessions. Typically, however, we devote scant attention to the needs of our brain, despite the fact that, during our waking hours, we rely on it completely. This chapter has focused on the ways that the capacity of our brain can be optimised for the purpose of problem solving in the FAE.

---

[8] Peale, N.V (1974), *op cit.* n.3.

Concentration is a key area of focus. Here, you must eliminate interruptions, get adequate relaxation, sleep well, eat healthily and take frequent study breaks. It is important too that you attempt case studies. This makes FAE problems more routine, so allowing your brain to provide solutions in a way that is faster and more reliable.

Positive thinking is another key component of problem solving. Always visualise your success in the FAE, keeping this picture in your head at all times. Finally, persevere and commit yourself to achieving that success.

PART III

Problem Solving:
The Planning Stage

Chapter 4. Defining the Problem

Problem solving in the FAE requires, in the first instance, that you **correctly identify the problem** that needs to be addressed. At all costs you want to avoid investing valuable time trying to resolve the wrong problem.

Consider the dilemma faced by the owners of a large high-rise apartment building where most of the tenants were staying only a short time before moving out. The building was ideally located, being close to shopping facilities and transport connections. The neighbourhood was also highly regarded from a security perspective. Yet, despite its obvious advantages, in recent months there had been a mass exodus of tenants.

The owners hired a consultancy group to investigate the matter. Having interviewed residents and former residents the consultants presented their findings. The problem, they said, was that "… the apartment lifts were too slow". The owners examined options involving the repair of the old lifts. Unfortunately this would not resolve the issue, so the installation of new lifts was also considered. While this would provide an effective solution, the cost was prohibitively high.

Resigned to the continuing loss of tenants, the owners decided to sell the building. Before they did so, however, they were approached by one tenant who suggested an alternative solution. The problem was not the speed of the lifts, she said, but the fact that tenants got bored waiting for them. She suggested that TV monitors should be installed in the lifts, which would provide up-to-date news stories and sports results. Piped music in the lobby areas might also help, as would some tasteful paintings and sculptures to engage the interest of tenants waiting for the lifts to arrive.

Her proposal worked and the exodus of tenants stopped, allowing the owners to abandon their plans to sell the building. This story underlines the importance of accurately defining a problem so that efforts to find a solution are focused in the right direction.

Defining Problems in the FAE

The typical FAE case study involves a business entity that has a number of issues. These issues are called **primary indicators**. To correctly identify the indicators, you will need to proceed as follows:

1. What is Your Role?

Your role will largely determine the issues that you will need to address. For example, the marketing director in a business will be concerned with increasing sales revenue. The production director's responsibility is to ensure that finished goods are available on schedule and within budget. The CEO, however, will be anxious to ensure that all parts of the business are integrated optimally.

Thus, **defining your role is always the first step in an FAE case**. Consider the Tidy Homes Group in **Supplement A** at the back of this book. Now I want you to study the first page of this FAE case and identify your role.

In the first paragraph, you are clearly identified as Susan Robson, financial accountant with the Tidy Homes Group. This appears to confirm your role, but it transpires that this is not the full story. Later, on the next page, you are informed that Cathy Crawford, the group finance director, is going to be out of the office for the next two weeks. During that time you will be taking over her role in relation to providing the Board with important information.

Thus, although you are nominally the group financial accountant, in this case you are effectively filling the role of Cathy Crawford. Therefore, you will be taking on whatever tasks would normally be carried out by the finance director. That is your role.

2. Identifying Indicators

Having established your role, it is now time to **identify the business issues** you will need to address – the primary indicators.

(a) Directed/Explicit Indicators Unlike the traditional style of other examination papers, an FAE case does not separately specify the requirements that the Examiner wishes you to address. Instead, you must become an **active participant** in the process. For example, this may involve attending a meeting with a client in your identified role. Following this meeting you should be in a position to determine what issues you will need to address. These may include issues that the client has expressed concern about, as well as others that, based on your professional judgement, will also need to be considered.

Directed indicators are those that are clearly signalled by the Examiner. They will become evident from careful study of each FAE case. Directed indicators are commonly found in conversations between people in the case and in the minutes of meetings.

Guidance is often provided at the end of the introductory text of a case as to where information on directed indicators can be located.

EXAMPLE 4.1: IDENTIFYING DIRECTED PRIMARY INDICATORS

Referring again to **Supplement A**, examine the Tidy Homes Group, and see if you can identify the **directed** indicators in this FAE case.

Solution

In your meeting with Cathy Crawford, Tidy Homes group finance director, you are informed that you will have to prepare information for a report that she will give to the Board in a month's time.

In the penultimate paragraph of the description of the meeting it states "Here is a copy of the Draft Board Minutes from last Friday's meeting (Appendix 3). Everything you need to address in the report should be in there."

This clearly indicates that most of what you need to address will be found in Appendix 3 of the Tidy Homes case. There we find the following primary indicators:

■ **Primary indicator 1:** Under point 2 it states "… it would be a prudent step to review the management information currently being produced within the Group to see what, if any, improvements could be made… CC should carry out a review and make any improvement recommendations she felt would be of benefit …".
■ **Primary indicator 2:** Under point 3 it states "… CC should prepare a report for the Board including a first draft of projections for the FY 2011 …".
■ **Primary indicator 3:** Under point 3 it states that the report should consider the "Possibility of closing Tidy Gardens Ltd".
■ **Primary indicator 4:** Point 3 also requires the report to outline the implications of the "Reduction of headcount of direct staff…". The implications of this headcount reduction will have to be considered.
■ **Primary indicator 5:** Point 3 also requires that a recommendation be made in respect of the "Outsourcing of the Group's IT function".
■ **Primary indicator 6:** The final paragraph of point 3, it was agreed "CC should also include in her report any tax … implications arising from the current situation of the business …".
■ **Primary indicator 7:** The final paragraph of point 3, it was agreed "CC should also include in her report any … financial reporting implications arising from the current situation of the business …".
■ **Primary indicator 8:** Point 4 requires that "… CC should include in her report recommendations as to what evidence THG would need to be able to supply to the auditors to ensure that an unqualified opinion could be given for the FY 2010 audit…".

An FAE Core comprehensive case requires that approximately seven to nine indicators be specified. Our analysis above has identified eight primary indicators. This suggests that we have identified most, if not all, of the indicators that are relevant to this FAE case.

PRACTICE EXERCISE 4.1: IDENTIFYING DIRECTED PRIMARY INDICATORS

Supplement B at the back of this book features the Platinum Software case. Examine this case now and see if you can identify the **directed** primary indicators.

(b) Self-directed/Implicit Indicators These are issues that the Examiner does **not explicitly request** in an FAE case. While not every case will have self-directed indicators, it is important to be able to recognise the 'flags' when they arise. For example, a client may outline a number of areas of his business that he wants advice on. A key feature of adding value to a client, however, is in identifying additional issues that need to be addressed. Self-directed indicators often emerge from an integration of the directed indicators and other information provided in the case.

For example, a client may be considering the importation of components from a supplier located in a low-cost economy. These components are currently manufactured in-house. Your analysis of the case identifies the following **directed** indicators:
■ computation of the cost of out-sourced components;
■ the impact of out-sourcing on company morale;
■ the cost of staff redundancies;
■ ensuring that the quality of out-sourced components is satisfactory;
■ alternative uses for the spare capacity created by the outsourcing of supplies;
■ financial reporting implications of closing the manufacturing division;
■ taxation implications of closing the manufacturing division;
■ consideration of the strategic implications of outsourcing; and
■ foreign exchange risk implications.

Further analysis and integration of the above issues may lead you to also identify the following **self-directed** indicators:
■ Risks arising from the remoteness of the supplier. These may include political, geographical and environmental risks. For example, many companies had supply-chain difficulties following the Japanese earthquake in 2011.
■ There may be ethical issues relating to the working conditions and wage levels of the new supplier's staff. Such issues have often been controversial for companies that source their supplies from low-cost economies.

These are important considerations that are not immediately apparent from one's first reading of a case. Indeed, issues relating to risk and ethics are often significant but are not always signalled as direct indicators in a case.

PRACTICE EXERCISE 4.2: IDENTIFYING SELF-DIRECTED PRIMARY INDICATORS

In **Supplement A** at the back of this book, examine the Tidy Homes Group and see if you can identify any **self-directed** indicators.

Issues to avoid Knowing what issues **not** to address is an essential part of any assignment. You may perceive certain matters as being important, but a client may not want assistance with them. From an FAE perspective, it is critical to identify issues that the Examiner wants you to steer clear of. Otherwise you may investigate an issue for up to 30 minutes before realising that it has been a complete waste of your time. However, you should exercise caution when a client suggests that some matter is irrelevant – using your professional knowledge you may decide that is not the case.

EXAMPLE 4.2: IDENTIFYING ISSUES TO AVOID

Brimeo Limited is currently considering the closure of its specialist wines' division. This division had been trading profitably for several years, but recently customers have been more interested in purchasing mid-range, less expensive wines. As marketing director of the company, you have been asked to make a presentation to the Board outlining the key issues that should be considered in making this decision. A sub-committee, chaired by the HR director, has been appointed to examine the impact of the proposed closure on the company's workforce.

Comment

As marketing director of Brimeo Limited, you should focus primarily on the marketing implications of the proposed closure of the specialist wines' division. You may, of course, extend your analysis to identify strategic, taxation or other consequences of closing the division. You should **not**, however, examine the HR implications of the closure. These are being examined by a separate sub-committee and, as far as you are concerned, HR is **an issue to avoid**.

PRACTICE EXERCISE 4.3: IDENTIFYING ISSUES TO AVOID IN THE TIDY HOMES CASE

Have another look at the Tidy Homes case in **Supplement A**. See if you can spot any issues to avoid.

PRACTICE EXERCISE 4.4: IDENTIFYING ISSUES TO AVOID IN THE PLATINUM SOFTWARE CASE

Now examine the Platinum Software case in **Supplement B** to see if you can spot any issues to avoid.

Summary

Before a problem can be solved it must first be properly defined. Often, large amounts of time are invested in trying to solve the wrong problem.

In FAE case studies, you must first know what your role is before you can determine what issues need to be addressed. Essentially, your role is **who you are** and **what your job specification is** in the case.

The issues that you must address are called primary indicators. There are two types of primary indicator:
1. indicators that are clearly identified in the case. These are called **directed** primary indicators; and
2. indicators that are not as clearly flagged. These are called **self-directed** primary indicators.

The majority of indicators in an FAE case are likely to be directed primary indicators. You should, however, be aware that some issues which are important may not be as clearly flagged by the Examiner. Sometimes these can be identified by establishing linkages between the directed primary indicators. Risk and ethical issues may also be important.

Finally, there may be issues in the case that the Examiner does **not** want you to address. These are **issues to avoid**, and you must be careful to identify them at an early stage so as not to waste valuable time.

The overall challenge of identifying the problems in each FAE case is outlined in **Figure 4.1**.

FIGURE 4.1: IDENTIFYING THE PROBLEM

Your Role (Identify)

Directed Indicators (Outline)	Self-directed Indicators? (Find)	Issues to Avoid (Time Wasters)

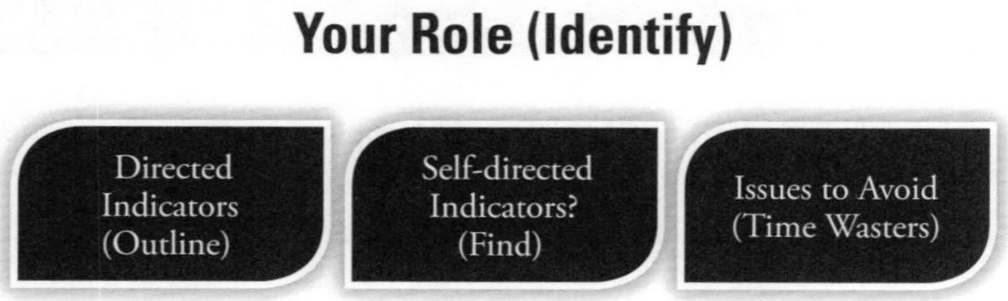

Chapter 5. Linking the Case Information and the Primary Indicators

Imagine that you have purchased a flat-pack desk which must be assembled. You begin by scratching your head, wondering what problem-solving approach you will employ. You decide to organise the various parts that come in the box. So you group the four legs together, likewise the three drawers, and the top of the desk that will have come packed as one piece. Then you arrange the nuts, bolts and screws into little like-sized groupings. When you have everything organised, you are ready to start assembling. You begin to follow the steps in the instructions leaflet which, if you're like me, you will probably understand after the desk has been assembled!

A similar approach is used when assembling the information in an FAE case. As outlined in **Chapter 4**, you will have begun by identifying your role and making a list of the primary indicators. You are therefore aware of the principal issues/problems that must be addressed. The next step is to **organise the information** provided in the case. This requires that you read the case in detail from the beginning. As you read, it will help to form a picture of the scene being described.

You have three objectives:
1. to link the information in the case with the already-identified primary indicators;
2. to identify any additional indicators (self-directed indicators) or issues to avoid that may have been overlooked; and
3. to form the 'big picture', so as to capture the key aspects of the case.

All three objectives are critical parts of the planning stage of the problem-solving process. The first two are addressed in this chapter, while the 'big picture' is covered in **Chapter 6**.

Linking the Information with the Primary Indicators

The purpose of having delayed a detailed reading of the case now becomes clear. Having already identified the primary indicators, every line of the case can now be considered in the context of its use in addressing those indicators. This is a focused reading of the case. However, had you read the case in detail **before** identifying the primary indicators it would have had less value.

As you read, you should record the link between points or paragraphs in the case and one or more primary indicators. This information can be effectively catalogued by making a note in the margin. For example, if a line in the case relates to primary indicator 2, a note in the margin might read 'PI 2'. Case exhibits or appendices should be similarly classified, each being identified as relating to one or more specific primary indicators.

Let us consider the application of this technique by re-visiting the Platinum Software case in **Supplement B**. Re-read the case now from the beginning. Using the primary indicators as your reference point (see the solution to **Practice Exercise 4.1** on page 111), underline or highlight relevant points in the case, making a note in the margin of the related primary indicator(s). When you have finished, check your approach by referring to **Supplement C** in this book.

"Jenkins – shouldn't you be in assembly?"

PRACTICE EXERCISE 5.1: LINKING THE CASE INFORMATION AND THE PRIMARY INDICATORS

Revisit the Tidy Homes Group in **Supplement A** and link the information in the case to the primary indicators.

Additional Indicators and Issues to Avoid

A detailed reading of an FAE case provides the opportunity to spot any additional indicators or issues to avoid that you may have overlooked previously. Primary indicators are sometimes located in close proximity, in the same appendix for example. However, this may not always be the case. A primary indicator could be found on its own, for example, in an individual exhibit.

During your detailed reading of a case, it is also critical that you spot any **issues to avoid** you may previously have overlooked. This will avoid an investment of time that would provide absolutely no return.

PRACTICE EXERCISE 5.2: ISSUES TO AVOID

Study the Tidy Homes case in **Supplement A**. You have previously established that "… any report should focus on the future and not historical performance," and that a high-level plan of action is already in place. Now see if you can spot any more issues to avoid.

Summary

Organising the information in a case is a critical part of the problem-solving process. In the FAE, this requires a detailed reading of each case study. This will enable you to link the information in the case to each issue/indicator that you need to address. You will also have the opportunity to spot any additional indicators or issues to avoid that you may have previously overlooked.

The part that this plays in the overall problem-solving process is outlined in **Figure 5.1**.

FIGURE 5.1: LINKING INFORMATION TO THE PRIMARY INDICATORS

Chapter 6. The Big Picture

As a plane approaches its destination, have you noticed how, from a window seat, you can often see an entire city? By night, the contrast between its bright lights and the surrounding darkness marks the city's boundaries even more clearly. Upon landing, however, you are enveloped by a mass of sprawling buildings, and your sky view soon becomes a distant memory.

Have you ever watched a near accident unfold, as a pedestrian walks into the path of an oncoming car, forcing the driver to brake suddenly? Or perhaps, from some overhead vantage point, you have seen people wander about in a maze, searching endlessly for an exit.

Sometimes, having an overview of the issues allows us to find a solution for even the most difficult of problems. This insight, this overall perspective that empowers us to become expert problem solvers, is called the 'big picture'. To become proficient at analysing and integrating information in the FAE, you must endeavour to see the 'big picture'.

FAE Case Studies and the Big Picture

What information is likely to make up the 'big picture' in an FAE case? The answer to this question will vary, but certain core information is likely to feature in most cases:
- What type of business is it? Consider issues such as:
  - whether public or private;
  - the industry sector;
  - whether it is expanding or contracting;
  - its principal shareholders; and
  - its management structure.
- What are the key indicators, i.e. what are the most critical issues facing the business?
- What links are there between the primary indicators?
- Are there any additional self-directed primary indicators such as significant risks or important ethical issues?

These issues are outlined in **Figure 6.1**.

FIGURE 6.1: THE BIG PICTURE

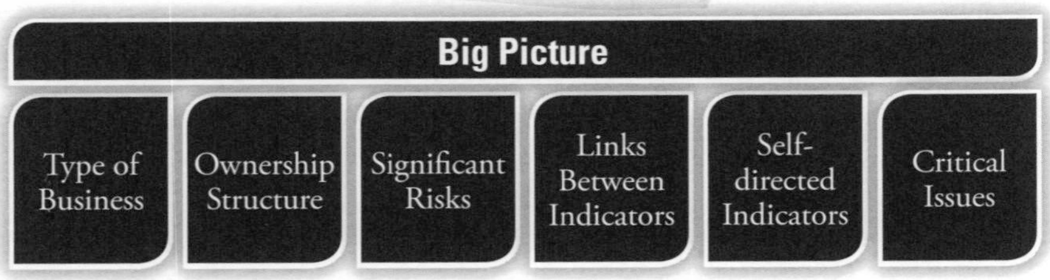

EXAMPLE 6.1: BIG PICTURE – THE TIDY HOMES GROUP

Let us revisit the Tidy Homes Group in **Supplement A**. The big picture in this case is illustrated as follows:

■ The Tidy Homes Group (THG) is a privately held group of companies.

■ THG is jointly owned by husband and wife, Mary and Peter Jones.

■ THG comprises Tidy Holdings (holding company), Tidy Homes (home cleaning), Tidy Offices (cleaning for businesses) and Tidy Gardens (gardening services).

■ Revenue is declining due to the economic downturn.

■ There has been a serious erosion of the group's cash balance.

■ THG has plans to downsize to reduce costs.

■ There is an urgent need to arrange financing to avoid bankruptcy. (**Lecture note**: this is a self-directed indicator.)

■ As THG is privately held, the only viable source of funding is debt. (**Lecture note**: this is an example of linking the information in the case.)

■ It is critical that THG receives a clean audit report. Otherwise it will be impossible to raise funding. (**Lecture note**: this is an example of linking indicators and also of identifying a key indicator.)

■ The following are **issues to avoid**:
  ■ analysis of historical performance; and
  ■ corporate governance issues.

An awareness of the big picture provides an overview insight into the Tidy Homes Group. Like the view from a plane or from a perch overlooking a maze, the big picture allows us to capture the essence of the Group, to identify the factors that are most critical to its future, and it provides an understanding of how the key issues interact with one another.

Review the Platinum Software case in **Supplement B** of this book and outline the big picture.

Summary

Having a clear understanding of a problem is an essential part of the problem-solving process. An overview enables the problem solver to determine the issues that are most critical to a business. It also permits linkages to be established between the primary indicators that must be addressed in the case. This overview is called the big picture, and it is an integral part of the FAE problem-solving technique.

Chapter 7. The Planning Stage – Overview

Planning is a critical part of the problem-solving process. In every FAE case, planning should consist of four parts:
1. establish what your role is;
2. identify the issues that must be addressed (i.e. the primary indicators);
3. relate all information to the primary indicators; and
4. outline the 'big picture'.

You have 30 minutes of reading time at the beginning of each FAE paper. You are not allowed to write in your answer book during that time, but planning should begin the first minute you have sight of the paper.

In the **Core Comprehensive** paper, the planning stage, including the reading time, should take approximately 60–80 minutes. Having completed the planning stage, you will then have approximately 3 hours and 30 minutes to implement your plan.

The total time allowed for the **Core Simulations** paper is also 4 hours, plus 30 minutes reading time. The total time, however, must be allocated between two case studies. A good strategy is to use approximately 35–45 minutes (including the 30 minutes' reading time) to plan the longer of the two case studies. The plan for the case should then be implemented. On completion of this case study, you should then use a similar approach for the second, taking approximately 25–35 minutes for its planning and the remaining time for its implementation. If both case studies are of an equal length, you should allow about 30–40 minutes' planning time for each one.

The total time allowed for the end-of-year **Elective** paper is also 4 hours, plus 30 minutes of reading time, but allocated between **two** cases. For this paper the best strategy is to use 30–40 minutes for the planning stage of one of the two cases. This plan should then be implemented. The second case should then be attempted using a similar approach.

The planning stage of the problem-solving process is illustrated in **Figure 7.1**.

FIGURE 7.1: PLANNING STAGE OF THE PROBLEM-SOLVING PROCESS

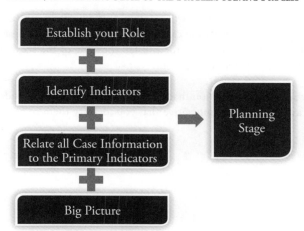

1. Establish what your Role is

The type of role that you play in an FAE case study can vary considerably. In one, you may be carrying out the duties of an external auditor or a financial consultant. In another, you might be the financial accountant in a public company or a private company's internal auditor. An FAE student must have a flexible mindset, one with the capacity to give attention to detail and the versatility to address issues across a range of business subjects.

Your first step in every FAE case study is to establish what your role is. This information will often be contained in the first page of a case. It will influence the way in which you analyse issues and the perspective from which you view them. For example, an internal auditor will be concerned with ensuring that a company's internal control system is effective in protecting its assets. The focus of an external auditor, however, is on being able to express an opinion on whether or not a company's financial statements give a true and fair view.

2. Identify the Issues that must be Addressed

Once you have determined your role, your next step is to identify what issues must be addressed. At this stage of the planning process you should **not** attempt a detailed reading of a case. Rather, you should only examine the case material to the extent that it is necessary to identify the issues that you must address.

In FAE case studies these issues are called primary indicators, and they can fall under two headings:

(a) Directed Indicators Directed indicators are issues that are clearly signalled in the case study. They are likely to arise from a request for information, a problem that must be resolved or some other reference to a matter that you must address.

(b) Self-directed Indicators These are issues that are **not explicitly requested,** but which you nonetheless decide are important. Self-directed indicators may relate to issues such as risk, security or ethics. They are likely to be far less numerous than directed indicators.

The Core Comprehensive case study will contain approximately seven to nine primary indicators, while each of the Simulation case studies will contain approximately three to five primary indicators. Each primary indicator will fall into one of the six major subject areas identified in the FAE Competency Statement.

A case may also contain an instruction that certain issues should not be addressed. These are called **'issues to avoid'**, and it is imperative that you identify them so as to avoid using up valuable time.

3. Link Information in the Case to the Primary Indicators

Once you have identified the primary indicators, you should read the case in detail. As you do so, you should consider how each sentence/paragraph can be used to address one or more primary indicators. You should also be on the lookout for additional primary indicators and issues to avoid.

4. Outline the Big Picture

The 'big picture' is the final stage of the planning process. Here you create an overview of the key information in the case. It will contain important information about the business, any critical decisions it faces and any linkages between the primary indicators previously identified. The integration of information in the 'big picture' may also enable you to identify a self-directed indicator that you had not spotted previously.

Summary

The planning stage is a critical part of the problem-solving process. It begins when you have sight of the examination paper and consists of four parts:
1. establish what your role is;
2. identify the issues that must be addressed (i.e. the primary indicators);
3. relate case information to the primary indicators; and
4. outline the 'big picture'.

It should be noted that only the material in your answer booklet will be marked by the Examiner. Any additional sheets, etc., that are inserted in the answer booklet are destroyed prior to marking.

On completion of the planning stage, you will be well positioned to address the primary indicators in each case. The implementation of your plan comes next and is covered in detail in **Part IV**.

Problem Solving:
The Implementation Stage

Chapter 8. Focus on Specifics

We have all listened to media interviews in which politicians and others engage in spin, skilfully avoiding questions posed by the interviewer. Such interviews are typically laced with general platitudes which are thought to appeal to a general audience.

An aspiring Chartered Accountant must possess a skill set precisely the opposite of that described above. In fact, the key skill demonstrated by a successful FAE student will be that of providing recommendations and solutions that are as **specific** as possible to the issue at hand.

Although the FAE is examined on an open book basis, a candidate is almost certain to fare better by adopting a closed book mindset. This involves using the specific information provided in a case, rather than relying on generic-style information that could be accessed in prescribed textbooks, course toolkits and other course materials. In fact, FAE candidates should generally have recourse to outside material only when all relevant information in the case has been used in providing one's answer.

In the exam, you may have access to study material that looks similar to what appears in an FAE case. You may even have a mock exam case that has covered similar ground. Remember, however, that you must address the specific circumstances of each case. Therefore, use the type of material described above with extreme caution.

The principle outlined above is clearly demonstrated in the Platinum Software case in **Supplement B** of this book. Let us consider it now.

EXAMPLE 8.1: FOCUS ON SPECIFICS – THE PLATINUM SOFTWARE CASE

A primary indicator, as identified in Appendix 2 of the Platinum Software case, is the "Need to identify and agree solutions to manage the currency risk as 10% of sales and 9% of product costs are now in US Dollars."

There are several alternative methods of managing exchange risk. However, the background information given makes specific reference to the following:
- "There are no foreign currency bank accounts"; and
- "The company always invoices clients overseas in their local currency".

Therefore, when outlining methods of managing exchange risk the first two areas to consider are:
- Setting up a US Dollar bank account will not be effective, as the company is receiving far more Dollars every month than it is paying out. Thus, this type of account would result in an ever-increasing Dollar balance accumulating in the account, thus exposing the company to the risk of the Dollar falling in value.

■ Invoicing US customers in Euros is also an option. However, this may not be feasible as it will result in the currency risk being transferred to the company's US customers, who will then be concerned about the risk of the Dollar weakening against the Euro.

Having addressed the methods mentioned in the case, it is now time to consider an alternative that may best fit the company's specific circumstances. Platinum Software is planning to expand significantly in the US, resulting in a substantial increase in Dollar receivables. It should therefore consider establishing a US base as part of its expansion plans, thereby generating Dollar expenses in running these operations. These Dollar expenses can then be offset against the company's Dollar receivables, thereby reducing the overall US Dollar exposure. This may be an effective means of handling the ongoing exchange risk (i.e. economic risk), as it will reduce the need to employ techniques to avoid exchange risk on a transaction-by-transaction basis. This method of exchange risk management is known as 'matching'.

We have now identified the risk management option that appears best suited to Platinum's circumstances. Finally, should time permit, we would consider other, more generic, alternatives; possibly referring to course material in order to identify the following:
■ forward purchase and sale of Dollars;
■ use of the money market; and
■ foreign currency options.

Conclusion

The following would be included as recommendations:
■ Neither a US Dollar bank account nor the invoicing of clients in Euros is likely to be a viable method of addressing Platinum's exchange risk. The first method is unsuitable and the latter is probably not practical.
■ The establishment of a US cost base as part of Platinum's expansion plans is likely to prove far more effective, particularly as it will play a strategic role in addressing the problem.
■ Other methods, such as the use of forward markets, money markets or foreign currency options may be useful as additional risk management methods for transaction-based purposes.

Analysis of Example 8.1

Example 8.1 demonstrates how to employ a focused approach to problem solving in the FAE. First, analyse the specific information provided in respect of a primary indicator. You should then consider additional information, specific to the circumstances and requirements of the business. For example, Platinum's expansion plans make it possible to use 'matching' by establishing a US production base. Finally, you can consider generic alternatives, such as the use of forward markets.

Example 8.1 also demonstrates the importance of having a detailed technical knowledge of the business disciplines that comprise the FAE. In this case, it was essential to be proficient in the area of foreign exchange risk management.

Read and Re-read the Primary Indicators

Each primary indicator (i.e. issue) is likely to comprise two or three lines. As you address a primary indicator, you should re-visit it frequently and read it afresh. Doing so may enable you to spot a nuance or direction that you did not notice previously. This will add depth to your answer. Re-reading a primary indicator will also make it more likely that you will stick to the point and provide information that is specific to the issue. The longer you continue to address an indicator without re-reading it, the more likely it is that your answer will become generic and less relevant.

Now re-visit the Parisian reference above, and read it again. Have you spotted the second 'the'?

Specialised Entities

It is quite common for an FAE case to be based on a specialist business or entity. While this may seem challenging, you should be reassured by the fact that you are not expected to have expert knowledge of such a business. Your answer must, however, reflect the specialist nature of the business. The key skill therefore is to apply general business principles to the particular circumstances of the business in question.

For example, a credit union will only lend to a customer when the lending officer believes that the loan will be repaid. As credit unions are 'not-for-profit' institutions, however, the lending criteria may be more accommodating of their members' needs. Also, as all loans are insured without any additional cost to the borrower, credit unions can be more flexible when a member is unable to service their loan commitments.

Thus, normal lending principles apply in relation to a specialised entity, such as a credit union. They are administered differently, however, as a credit union operates on a 'not-for-profit' basis. Similarly, a private hospital will have to balance the competing objectives of customer care and profitability. So, although normal commercial principles apply, they must be balanced with the need to ensure that patients are treated with dignity and respect.

When dealing with a specialist entity in an FAE case, the challenge is to apply your business knowledge in a way that reflects the specific circumstances of the entity in question.

PRACTICE EXERCISE 8.1: SPECIALIST ENTITY – THE AMY CASE

One of the Core Simulation cases in the Autumn 2011 FAE concerned a charity called "Amy". This case is included as **Supplement D** in this book and contains the following primary indicator:

"In light of the charity's specific objectives, you have also been asked to identify suitable KPIs that can be presented to the Board at its next meeting."

Read the Amy simulation now and outline how you would address the above primary indicator. A suggested solution is provided in **Solutions to Practice Exercises** at the back of this book.

Summary

A focus on specifics is a prerequisite for success in the FAE. An entity's exact circumstances must be addressed when dealing with each primary indicator. A key skill, therefore, is the application of your professional knowledge in a way that is highly focused. The use of generic information is of limited value and, although the FAE is an open book examination, it requires a closed book mindset.

The same mindset extends to cases involving a **specialist** entity, such as a charity, a credit union or a private hospital. While general business principles are relevant, they must be applied in a way that fully reflects the particular objectives and circumstances of this type of entity.

When addressing a primary indicator, you should revisit the information provided in the case study several times during your planning and writing stages. This will ensure you understand it fully and will enable you to stay focused and direct when providing your answer. A good rule of thumb is to check that each paragraph you write references the case study, client or situation. If it does not you are in danger of providing a generic answer.

Chapter 9. Knowledge and the Three Dimensions

An FAE candidate is expected to apply knowledge in three dimensions. This requires the exercise of the following skills:
- fundamental skills;
- value-adding skills; and
- advisory skills.

Fundamental Skills

These are the core skills that every Chartered Accountant is expected to demonstrate. They include the ability to identify and describe problems, and to effect calculations involving areas such as tax computations, variance analysis and the preparation of financial statements.

Value-adding Skills

Having executed the core skills (e.g. preparation of a draft tax computation before a client's year end), a Chartered Accountant should then meet with a client to explore further issues arising. For example, the purchase of equipment before the financial year end could optimise the use of capital allowances. The discussion could also include pensions and retirement planning and relevant capital acquisitions tax issues.

By assisting a client in this way, a Chartered Accountant is adding value, having already demonstrated the core skill of preparing the client's draft tax computation.

See **Chapter 11** for a further discussion of value-adding skills.

Advisory Skills

These are high-level skills that require a Chartered Accountant to exercise his/her professional judgement. They involve providing a client with conclusions, recommendations and advice based on the alternatives identified at the value-adding stage. For example, one might recommend to a client which of the tax planning options would be most appropriate to his/her circumstances.

See **Chapter 12** for a further discussion of advisory skills.

The relationship between the three dimensions of knowledge is outlined in **Figure 9.1**.

FIGURE 9.1: THREE DIMENSIONS OF KNOWLEDGE

Skills required of a Chartered Accountant	How Skill is Exercised	Contribution to Competence*
Fundamental	■ Identify ■ Describe ■ Explain ■ Calculate	The exercise of fundamental skills will generally contribute to 'Basic Competence' and 'Competent' ratings.
Value-adding	■ Assess ■ Analyse ■ Expand ■ Compare ■ Integrate ■ Interpret ■ Outline alternatives ■ Identify need for additional information	Having satisfactorily demonstrated fundamental skills, value-adding skills will generally contribute to 'Competent' and 'Highly Competent' ratings.
Advisory	■ Outline implications of ■ Advise ■ Conclude ■ Recommend	Having satisfactorily demonstrated fundamental and value-adding skills, displaying advisory skills will generally contribute to 'Competent' and 'Highly Competent' ratings.

* See **Chapter 2** for details of FAE competence levels.

Summary

An FAE candidate is expected to develop a skillset capable of applying business knowledge on three dimensions:
■ fundamental skills;
■ value-adding skills; and
■ advisory skills.

The appropriate combination of these skills will significantly enhance one's ability to demonstrate competence in the FAE.

Chapter 10. Exhibits and Calculations

A little five-year old closed the car door and fastened his seat belt.

"What did you learn today, Timmy?" enquired his mother, driving away from the school and heading for home.

"Two and two, that son of a bitch is four."

"Did your teacher say that?" asked his mother, so stunned that she almost crashed the car.

"She said two and two, that son of a bitch is four," replied Timmy, and he began reciting it with enthusiasm from the back of the car.

The following day, Timmy's mother decided to confront his teacher.

"He said what?" asked the teacher incredulously.

Timmy's mother repeated the profanity, and the teacher laughed heartily. When she had regained her composure, she explained what she had actually said:

"…two and two, the sum of which is four."

Calculations are central to most of what a Chartered Accountant does. Whether computing a company's profit and tax liability, details of variances, the net present value (NPV) of a project or the cost of a product, an accountant is constantly working with numbers. Computations are time-consuming, however, and like Timmy's mum, one can easily be led astray.

The key point is that **before** you do a computation you must know where it will take you. Do nothing unless you know precisely what a calculation will be used for. It is essential to realise that computations are just a means to an end. For example, a project's NPV will be critical in deciding whether it should be undertaken. An unfavourable sales price variance will require a review of a firm's pricing policy or perhaps a re-appraisal of its budgeted selling prices. A firm's weighted average cost of capital (WACC) provides the hurdle rate used to evaluate capital projects that, for a particular firm, are typical in terms of its risk profile.

'Use it or lose it' is a phrase commonly associated with rugby. It signals a warning from the referee that the team in possession must use the ball or he will award a scrum to the opposing team. 'Use it or lose it' also applies in the FAE. Having spent time doing a calculation, you **must use** the work that you have done, or the benefit will be lost. For example, based on an analysis of cash flows, you may conclude that a company should upgrade its IT system. You must communicate that conclusion to whomever you are reporting. In doing so, you should supplement your advice with relevant qualitative points.

You may advise, for example, that the new IT system should initially run in parallel with the old system. You will also stress the importance of data security during the changeover process. Therefore, used appropriately, calculations are a means to an end. What matters most, however, is that you use those computations to deliver a professional service that will add value to your client.

Using Exhibits

FAE cases typically contain one or more exhibits. Exhibits might include information such as a set of financial statements, a copy of board minutes, details of product costings or project cash flows, a list of variances, or a summary of a firm's accounting policies. Each exhibit should be evaluated in the context of how it can be used to address one or more of the primary indicators. This linkage must be established **before** you commence any time-consuming computational work. The steps are outlined sequentially in **Figure 10.1**.

FIGURE 10.1: USING EXHIBITS AND CALCULATIONS

When examining exhibits, you should be vigilant for any items that are significant or unusual. These may include:

■ high value items;
■ items involving a material change between periods;
■ amounts for which additional details or explanations are provided;
■ items that could be significant for legal or ethical reasons;
■ anything that could affect a company's going concern status; and
■ items that could result in a qualified audit opinion.

PRACTICE EXERCISE 10.1: POSSIBLE CLOSURE OF TIDY GARDENS

The possibility of closing Tidy Gardens Ltd is a primary indicator in the Autumn 2010 Core Comprehensive case (see **Supplement A** of this book).

Study Appendices 4(A) and 4(B) of that case, and outline how the information contained therein can be used in deciding whether or not to close Tidy Gardens.

Linking Calculations and Primary Indicators

The nature of a primary indicator will usually determine the type of calculation that is required in an FAE case. Figure 10.2 provides some examples of primary indicators and the calculations required to address them.

FIGURE 10.2: LINKING CALCULATIONS AND PRIMARY INDICATORS

Primary Indicator	Typical Calculation Required
Evaluating an investment opportunity	Net present value
Addressing a solvency problem	Forecast cash flow
Managing risk (interest rate/foreign exchange)	Alternative risk management strategies
Purchase/sale of a business	Share valuation
Addressing a group profitability issue	Divisional contribution analysis

Summary

The preparation of calculations is a fundamental skill of a Chartered Accountant. It is an area in which an FAE student will be expected to demonstrate competency. However, calculations are time-consuming and in the FAE they should only be undertaken when it is clear that they are necessary in order to address a primary indicator. Calculations are a means to an end, and it is essential that one's results are used as the basis for a conclusion or recommendation. It is also important that one's findings are supported by appropriate qualitative analysis.

Chapter 11: Achieving Depth

Introduction

A man was walking in a meadow when he happened upon a hole. Wanting to see how deep it was, he threw a pebble in the hole and waited for it to land. Hearing nothing, he picked up a larger stone and tossed it in the hole. Once again there was no sound. Scratching his head, he wondered what to do. Nearby, he found a medium-sized rock, and lifting it up he dropped it in the hole. He pricked up his ears and listened intently but heard nothing. Finding a huge boulder some distance away, he hauled it along the ground and levered it into the hole. He waited patiently, but once again he heard nothing.

The man sat on the ground exhausted. Suddenly, he saw a goat running towards him at full speed. He leapt aside and the goat flew past and jumped headlong into the hole. The man sat down again. Some time later, a farmer came walking up.
"Have you seen a goat?" he asked.
"No," replied the man, fearing that he might be blamed for the goat's disappearance down the hole.
"Well, he can't be gone far," said the farmer. "Sure, I had him tied to a massive rock."

To the man in this story the question of depth proved unfathomable. Had he sought to broaden his problem-solving approach he may have had more success. By persevering with larger stones, however, each time the problem grew bigger and the consequences (especially for the goat!) more serious.

As outlined in **Chapter 2**, a candidate must demonstrate proficiency on three levels in the FAE Core: sufficiency, depth and breadth. The requirement to demonstrate depth is an essential one in Business Leadership and Financial Accounting and Reporting. Achieving depth, while not required to meet the **minimum** standard in the other subject areas, **is** needed to increase one's chances of satisfying the FAE **sufficiency** requirement. Thus, the demonstration of depth is a prerequisite for success in the FAE.

Demonstrating Depth

Imagine that a sudden gush of water comes through the ceiling as you sit on the couch watching television. You shriek with fright and, after gathering your thoughts, you sprint to the mains switch and shut off the water supply. The solution is as automatic as the problem, and it requires little thought or consideration.

Now imagine that you are sitting on the same couch, and you notice a drop land on the floor in the centre of the room. Your eyes are drawn upwards, and you stare intently as a drop gradually grows in size, its weight eventually causing it to lose its hold on the ceiling.

You drift back to the television and laugh at something or other that appears on the screen. After a while your attention returns to the ceiling. A number of questions go around in your head:

■ What has caused the leak?
■ How can it be fixed?
■ How much damage has it caused?
■ What is the likelihood of other leaks elsewhere in the house?
■ Should you submit an insurance claim to cover the cost of repairing the damage?

There are many issues to be addressed in the case of a 'drip-drip' leak. For example, the leak may have been caused by a broken roof tile, a burst pipe or an overflow from the water tank in your attic. The method of fixing the leak will depend largely on its cause, but there may, in any event, be a number of alternatives. To assess the damage, you will need to go upstairs and possibly also carry out an inspection of the attic. The question of locating other leaks will require a visual inspection throughout your house. Submitting an insurance claim will provide a cash inflow, but the cost of your premium will increase if you decide to forfeit your no-claims bonus.

The 'drip-drip' leak requires you to think in depth about the nature of the problem and how it can be solved. There are several variables to be considered, some of which are interlinked or interdependent. The solution to the 'drip-drip' leak requires the application of depth in the problem solver's thinking. In this way, it is more indicative of the challenges you will face in the FAE, than that provided by the sudden gush of water which points to an immediate, albeit temporary, solution.

Methods of Demonstrating Depth

Depth in the FAE can be demonstrated by gradually unwrapping the different layers of a problem. This requires that you organise your thought process in a logical, consistent, and yet creative manner. A variety of approaches can be employed, and they include the following:
1. a cradle-to-grave/chronological approach;
2. a conflicting perspectives approach; and
3. an establishing linkages approach.

1. Cradle-to-grave/Chronological Approach

A cradle-to-grave approach examines an issue from commencement to termination. A chronological approach traces the evolution of an issue over a period of time. Both approaches are broadly similar and they are considered together for the purpose of achieving depth in the FAE.

A primary indicator might, for example, require that you outline how an asset should be accounted for. Using a cradle-to-grave approach, you would proceed as follows:
■ at the time of purchase (consider recognition criteria, estimation of useful life, decommissioning costs and residual value);
■ during the asset's life (consider annual depreciation/amortisation, choice of cost or valuation model, accounting for revaluations and impairments, and revision of asset's useful life);
■ at the end of the asset's life (consider presenting as an asset held for sale, abandonment or disposal, and disclosure of profit or loss on sale).

It is critical, of course, that you only consider the above points to the extent that they relate to the specific asset in question. In respect of **land** for example, which normally has an infinite useful 'life', at the time of purchase it will only be necessary to consider recognition criteria. During the 'life' of the land, it will only be necessary to consider the choice of valuation model and how to account for revaluations and impairments.

PRACTICE EXERCISE 11.1: OUTSOURCING PROPOSAL

A company is considering outsourcing the manufacture of a component used in its production process. Outline what factors should be considered in making this decision.

---

2. Conflicting Perspectives Approach

Stakeholder theory maintains that business entities have a responsibility to other parties as well as to shareholders. Depth can be achieved by examining an issue from different perspectives, as long as those perspectives involve parties that can justifiably be regarded as stakeholders of the business.

PRACTICE EXERCISE 11.2: PROPOSED TAKEOVER

Rhyme Limited is currently the subject of a takeover bid. The chief executive, who stands to benefit substantially, is in favour of accepting the offer. The current year's financial statements are due to be announced shortly and the chief executive wants the profit figure to be as high as possible, with a view to ensuring that the bidder completes the deal. He has proposed minimising accruals and opting for accounting policies that will maximise profit.

In your capacity as the finance director of Rhyme Limited you have been asked to advise the Board.

---

3. Establishing Linkages Approach

When a detective arrives at a crime scene, the first step is to gather evidence. In the following weeks witnesses will be interviewed to try and identify a suspect. The detective will then seek to establish links between the suspect and the crime using techniques such as DNA testing, fingerprinting, CCTV images and phone records. If any of these help the case, the detective will prepare a 'book of evidence' that will be used when the case comes to trial.

In a similar way, a doctor will examine the links between a patient's symptoms and the anatomy of an illness. An athlete will study food supplements and training methods to optimise his/her performance. Social networking sites routinely seek to establish links between users as a way of growing their businesses.

Likewise, establishing links is important if you want to achieve depth in the FAE. Business issues are often related and you should always be on the lookout for an opportunity to link the issues in a case.

PRACTICE EXERCISE 11.3: ESTABLISHING LINKS

Morse Limited is a manufacturer of fireplaces. The company, which is family owned, has a long-established tradition of appointing its Board members from the ranks of its skilled craftsmen.

"It's a way of ensuring that quality comes first," says Frank Morse, the company's major shareholder. Over the last two years, Morse Limited has seen its share of the fireplace market decline as other suppliers compete with cheaper but inferior quality alternatives.

You have been asked to advise the Board as to what course of action it should pursue in order to arrest the company's decline.

Summary

FAE candidates must demonstrate proficiency on three levels: sufficiency, depth and breadth. While depth is a requirement in its own right, being proficient in this respect will also help in terms of demonstrating sufficiency. Depth, therefore, has a dual role to play in the FAE.

This chapter has focused on the ways in which you can demonstrate depth in the FAE. The key requirement is that you organise your thinking in a way that is logical and consistent, but at the same time develop your capacity to think creatively. Depth, therefore, requires an approach that is more subtle and varied than merely increasing the size of stone that you drop down a hole.

Three approaches are outlined as examples of ways in which depth can be achieved:
1. the cradle-to-grave/chronological approach;
2. the conflicting perspectives approach; and
3. the establishing linkages approach.

① START TO FINISH
② DIFFERENT ANGLES
③ LINKING INDICATORS

These approaches are not intended to be exhaustive in terms of the methods you can employ to demonstrate depth; nor are they mutually exclusive. You can, for example, establish linkages between issues while also exploring them on a cradle-to-grave basis. What is important is that you integrate your knowledge in a way that is comprehensive, creative and consistent.

It is important to point out that depth does not equal length. Rather than writing at length on a particular point, you are more likely to demonstrate depth by making several points and employing a technique such as 'cradle-to-grave' to develop an issue.

Chapter 12. Be Decisive!

"Have you always found it difficult to make decisions?" asked the doctor.
"Well, yes and no", replied the patient, finding it hard to make up his mind.

Unfortunately, sitting on the fence is a luxury that an FAE student cannot afford. In a typical FAE case you will be required to make several decisions. For example:

- the possible closure of a division;
- whether to acquire a target company;
- whether a capital investment opportunity should be undertaken; and
- the most optimal transfer price.

In addressing these questions, you may raise several more. Rudyard Kipling put it well in his poem, "The Elephant's Child":

> "I keep six honest serving-men
> (They taught me all I knew);
> Their names are What and Why and When
> And How and Where and Who."

Questions such as these may help you to comprehensively examine a primary indicator. You might identify a number of alternative courses of action, each with advantages that would cause you to favour it. Having considered all the alternatives, however, you **must ultimately choose only one.**

Your choice may depend on several factors. Maybe one investment opportunity has a higher NPV than another, or perhaps it has significant qualitative advantages that compensate for having a lower NPV. Maybe it is the best strategic fit for the company's overall operations, or perhaps it involves a lower level of risk than other higher-NPV projects.

Regardless of the basis for your conclusion, it is critical that you provide a recommendation to whoever has requested your advice. In business, most information is prepared for decision-making purposes; this is certainly the case in the FAE. You may be reporting to your audit partner, to the client's chief executive or to its board of directors. Each will expect you to provide the information and the advice required for whatever decision they must take.

A key aspect of delivering a professional service is that the advice you provide is consistent with the underlying facts. Thus, it is critical in the FAE that your analysis is consistent with your computations, and that your advice is consistent with your analysis. This is illustrated in **Figure 12.1**.

FIGURE 12.1: DELIVERING A PROFESSIONAL SERVICE

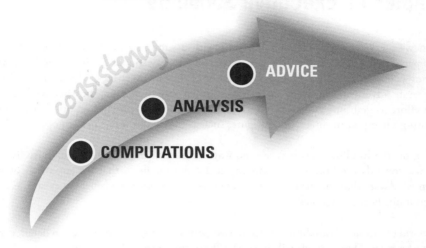

ADVICE

ANALYSIS

COMPUTATIONS

consistency

PRACTICE EXERCISE 12.1: ACCOUNTING POLICY CHOICE

Jupiter Limited has just acquired its first investment property for €4.2 million. You have been asked, in your role as an audit senior in Light, Torch, Byrne & Co., to outline what accounting treatment the company can adopt in respect of the newly acquired investment property.

You are aware that Jupiter operates an incentive scheme, whereby management bonuses are based on the company's annual profit figure. Jupiter revalues its land and buildings assets, as permitted by IAS 16 *Property, Plant and Equipment*. The finance director has expressed concern, however, regarding any unfavourable tax consequences of carrying investment property at a revalued amount.

Summary

The provision of a professional service demands that advice must add value, in terms of providing a client with a specific recommendation, supported by rigorous analysis, and with all significant assumptions clearly stated. Ultimately, it is the client who will make the decision, but the role of the Chartered Accountant is to recommend the alternative that is most appropriate to a client's circumstances.

The same principle applies in the FAE, and you should always ensure that you complete your answer to each primary indicator with a clear recommendation or conclusion.

Chapter 13. Executive Summary

The news on TV or radio invariably opens with a summary of the headlines. On their front page, newspapers flag the biggest stories of the day. Books do it on the back page, drawing you in by revealing an appealing outline of the plot. Websites, which rely on visitors to generate advertising income, operate in a similar way by flagging provocative headlines in an effort to grab our attention. Corporate annual reports provide yet another example, disclosing a five-year summary of key figures such as EPS and revenue in their opening pages.

Dining on the headlines has become the way of the modern world. In our busy lives we gravitate towards the bottom line, hoping to learn enough so that we appear to be well informed. Aware that the devil is in the detail, we decide to live a heavenly existence as we go about our hectic schedules.

The world of business is no different. Executives, not wanting to be swamped in detail, expect you to be brief. "How much will it cost? What's the bottom line?" they ask impatiently, demanding a one-line response. In business reports, the reader's eye is drawn to what has become known as the **executive summary**. Mulling over the findings and recommendations, they will open the main report only if they want to know more.

Consider the story of the family who arrive in London having lived in a rural area for many years. They go shopping in Harrods, and the youngest son asks his father if he will take him to see the toy section. His father takes the boy's hand, and as they walk along they see two metal doors in the middle of a long wall.
"What's that?" asks the little boy.
His father shakes his head and, as they watch, the doors open and an elderly lady steps inside. Their gaze remains fixed on the doors, and a minute later they re-open and a beautiful young lady steps out.
"Get your mother, son," says the man.

Now imagine that you are stepping into a lift on the 20th floor of a building. Your audit partner is standing alongside and you have 30 seconds to brief him/her on the main issues to be discussed with a client. The lift begins to descend and, drawing a breath, you begin what is known as the 'elevator pitch'.

In the FAE, an executive summary takes on the role of an elevator pitch and, like the lift in Harrods, it has the potential to change the appearance of your script. Admittedly, the examining team will read everything that you write, but an executive summary provides a focal point, allowing you to showcase your key findings and recommendations. For a modest investment of time, you can transform your script into a business report that will add value for your client, and provide something that your client will be happy to pay for.

If the action required of you in the case study would benefit from an executive summary, you should leave space at the beginning for its inclusion. It should contain a synopsis of the main issues you have addressed along with your key findings and recommendations. It is best to complete the executive summary as you go, taking a moment to add to it as you complete each primary indicator. In total, an executive summary should be no longer than one to two pages but, by emphasising your professionalism, it will punch beyond its length and prove a useful ally in your quest to display competence. Note, however, that the executive summary should always be proportionate to the length of the case or solution.

See the sample executive summary in **Supplement E** of this book.

Summary

An executive summary has the potential to transform your answer into a professionally prepared report. Include an executive summary at the front of each FAE case, outlining the principal issues you have addressed and your key findings. An executive summary should be no longer than a page or two and should be relevant and proportionate to the type of case you are working on.

Chapter 14. The Implementation Stage – Overview

Having completed the planning stage of the problem-solving process, you are ready to write your answer in each FAE case study. This is the point at which the work you have already done will begin to pay dividends. The implementation stage of the problem-solving process is outlined in **Figure 14.1**.

FIGURE 14.1: THE IMPLEMENTATION STAGE

1. Focus on Specifics

The exact circumstances of a business must be addressed when dealing with each primary indicator. The use of generic information is of limited value, and although the FAE is an open book examination, it requires a closed book mindset.

When addressing a primary indicator, you should re-visit it frequently, to ensure that you understand it fully, and to stay focused and direct in your answer.

2. Achieving Depth

To demonstrate depth, you must organise your thinking in a way that is logical and consistent. You must also be able to think creatively. Three approaches to achieving depth were outlined in **Chapter 11**:
1. the cradle-to-grave/chronological approach;
2. the conflicting perspectives approach; and
3. the establishing linkages approach.

These approaches are neither exhaustive nor mutually exclusive in terms of the methods that you can employ to demonstrate depth. What is important is that you integrate your knowledge in a way that is comprehensive, creative and consistent.

It is important to point out that depth does not equal length. Rather than writing at length on a particular point, you are more likely to demonstrate depth by making several points, and by employing a technique such as the 'cradle-to-grave' approach to develop an issue.

3. Be Decisive!

A Chartered Accountant does not have the luxury of being able to sit on the fence and outline many alternative courses of action. The provision of a professional service demands that advice must add value in terms of providing a client with a specific recommendation, supported by rigorous analysis and with all significant assumptions clearly stated. Ultimately, it is the client who will make the decision, but the role of the Chartered Accountant is to recommend the alternative that is most appropriate to a client's circumstances.

The same principle applies in the FAE, and you should always ensure that you complete your answer to each primary indicator with a clear recommendation or conclusion.

4. Using Exhibits and Calculations

Calculations can be time consuming and time is a scarce commodity in all of the FAE papers. So before you embark on any lengthy computation, you must know precisely where it will lead you. If you are not sure how a calculation will be used to address a primary indicator – don't do it!

Once you complete an essential computation, don't abandon it and move on to something else, even if you are under time pressure. Always use the result as the basis for a recommendation, advice or a conclusion.

5. Executive Summary

An executive summary provides you with a focal point, allowing you to showcase your key findings and recommendations. An executive summary should appear at the front of each FAE case that you complete, and should summarise your key findings and recommendations. It should be no longer than a page or two, and it should summarise your key findings and recommendations.

Summary

Having completed the planning stage, you are ready to write your answer to each FAE case. This involves the implementation of your plan and it consists of the following steps:
■ focusing on specifics;
■ achieving depth;
■ being decisive;
■ using exhibits and calculations to address primary indicators; and
■ preparing an executive summary where relevant.

PART V

Business Developments

Chapter 15. Keeping Up-to-date

Every professional should be fully informed about their chosen area of expertise. A client's needs can extend across a broad range of business areas, and a Chartered Accountant should be up-to-date with global and domestic economic developments. An awareness of current events and their implications can also assist in demonstrating competence in the FAE. While the cases require a candidate to focus on the circumstances of a particular business, every entity operates against the backdrop of broader economic events and an awareness of these can inform and enhance the advice that you provide to a client.

You should, therefore, keep up-to-date with major developments in the business world. Reading the business pages on a daily basis is a useful habit, with the *Financial Times* being a particularly good source of information. **Figure 15.1** demonstrates how you can track economic events and analyse their potential implications for business.

FIGURE 15.1: POSSIBLE IMPLICATIONS OF SOME NATIONAL AND INTERNATIONAL EVENTS

Event	Possible Implications
Political instability, e.g. crises and civil wars in the Middle East and North Africa or within Europe	Increase in oil price Volatility in financial markets
Rise in oil and commodity prices	Higher transport and food costs for businesses Incentive to locate supply chain locally Increase in online sales, due to higher consumer transport costs Pressure on the euro Less revenue buoyancy in affected countries, due to austerity measures imposed by ECB Possible loss of 12.5% corporation tax rate in ROI, with severe consequences for foreign direct investment
Inflation rising globally	Governments increase interest rates to stem inflationary pressures (i.e. monetary policy measures)
Interest rates increasing	Lower profits Less borrowing by businesses Companies more likely to use own equity as consideration for acquisitions

Event	Possible Implications
Natural disasters, e.g. the Japanese earthquake in 2011	Companies review policy of locating supply chain on a remote basis in cheaper economies
Rationalisation of financial services sector	Less competition between banks and, thus, higher borrowing costs for business
Scarcity of funding	Capital rationing becomes a more relevant factor and, therefore, increased focus on NPV
Falling property prices	Negative equity for businesses holding property assets Impairment losses in income statement Property less valuable as collateral for borrowing purposes
Falling consumer spending	More pressure on businesses to compete on price and quality
Rising unemployment	Increased burden falling on the employed, as governments will be forced to resort to tax increases (fiscal policy)
Downgrading of US credit rating	Increased demand for gold and other precious metals Dollar could lose its standing as the world's most important currency Pressure on the US to increase interest rates in order to reduce lending and cut its deficit Less chance of further quantitative easing in the US

Summary

FAE candidates should keep up-to-date with economic developments and their implications for businesses. Enhancing your knowledge in this way can be useful in demonstrating depth in the FAE. It also represents a valuable lifelong investment in advancing your future career.

PART VI

Overall Summary

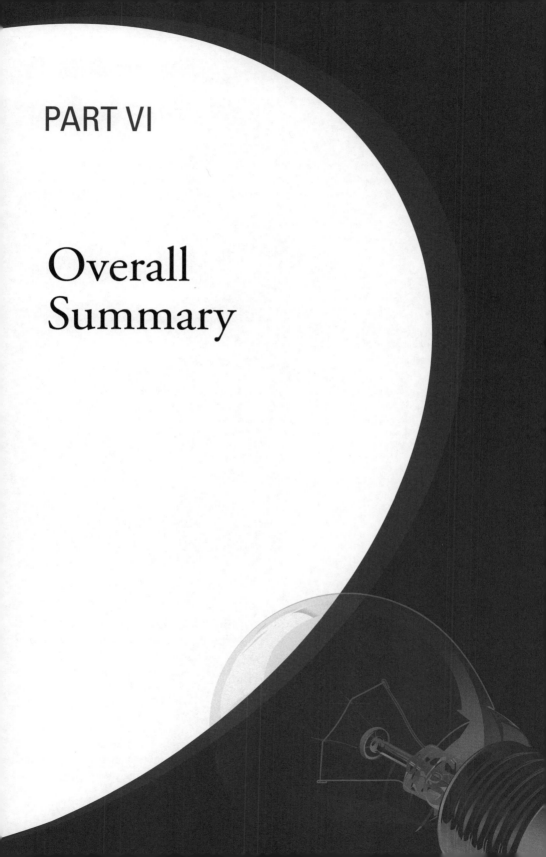

Overall Summary

Chapter 16: Overall Summary

> A rabbit was once lost in a dense wood, when he came upon a wise old owl
> sitting on a tree branch.
> "Please help me, owl. How can I get out of the wood?"
> "Easy", said the owl. "Just grow wings and fly out, as I do."
> "But how can I grow wings?" asked the rabbit.
> Looking at the rabbit disdainfully, the owl said, "Don't bother me with the
> details. I only advise on strategy."

Unlike the wise old owl, an FAE student must be willing to advise on matters of detail, as
well as being knowledgeable on broader issues such as strategy. In fact, an FAE candidate is
required to be proficient in numerous business disciplines. An FAE candidate is also expected
to integrate material from these disciplines when addressing business issues.

The important issues that arise in FAE cases are called **primary indicators**. Addressing these
issues and resolving them satisfactorily is an exercise in problem solving. The objective of
this book is to provide FAE students with an effective problem-solving approach that will
enable them to resolve issues and report in a way that demonstrates the professionalism
expected of a Chartered Accountant.

For candidates to be successful in the FAE, they must satisfy two key prerequisites:
1. possess the required level of technical knowledge across the syllabus; and
2. apply that knowledge in a specific way to the circumstances presented in each FAE case.

Overview of the Problem-solving Approach

The problem-solving approach that has been set out in this book is now summarised as
follows:

Know the Requirements
The **structure** and method of **assessment** of the FAE are outlined in **Part 1** of this book.
You should ensure that you are fully conversant with these rules. To pass the FAE, you must
demonstrate competence on three levels: sufficiency, depth and breadth.

Lay the Foundations
"A focused brain always delivers power." This statement from **Chapter 3** emphasises the
importance of maximising your brain power. This requires that you develop your capacity to
concentrate; that you simulate exam conditions; that you think positively at all times; that
you commit yourself to the FAE; and that you persevere with that commitment.

Problem Solving – the Planning Stage

You must begin by establishing what your **role** is in each FAE case. You should then identify the **primary indicators**. These can comprise directed primary indicators, self-directed indicators, and issues to avoid, which are issues that must not be addressed.

You should then **read the case in detail** and establish how each piece of information, including exhibits, can be used to address the primary indicators. You should complete the planning stage of each case by creating the '**big picture**', which should capture the key aspects of the business and the challenges facing it. The planning stage is summarised in **Figure 16.1**.

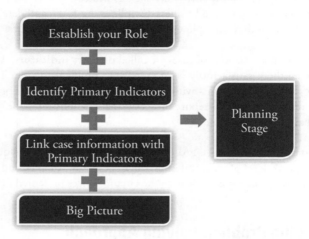

FIGURE 16.1: THE PLANNING STAGE

Having completed the planning stage, you are now ready to write your answer.

Problem Solving – the Implementation Stage

You must deal with the exact circumstances of a business when addressing each primary indicator. **Specific** points are required and offering generic information is of very little value.

You should only carry out time-consuming **calculations** if you are certain that your results can be used to address a primary indicator. Computations are usually based on one or more exhibits that are provided as part of an FAE case.

Demonstrating **depth** is a mandatory requirement in its own right and it will also help you to satisfy the sufficiency requirement of the FAE. To demonstrate depth, you must organise your thinking in a way that is logical and consistent. Rather than writing a lengthy point, you should aim to develop an issue by making several succinct points. **Chapter 11** suggests three approaches which may be employed in order to demonstrate depth: cradle-to-grave, taking conflicting perspectives, and establishing linkages.

You must be **decisive**. While it is important to consider all viable alternatives, you must ultimately decide which option is best. You must reach a conclusion, and include definitive advice in your report, taking care to note any key assumptions that underlie your recommendation.

Where appropriate you should attach an **executive summary** to the front of your case solution. This should be no more than a page or two in length and you can update it as you finish each primary indicator. The executive summary should identify the main issues faced by a business along with your key findings and recommendations.

The implementation stage is summarised in **Figure 16.2**.

FIGURE 16.2: THE IMPLEMENTATION STAGE

Chapter 17. Step-by-step Guide to an FAE Case Study

This chapter provides a focused synopsis of the approach set out in this book. It is intended as a reference point for students who have read and understood the ideas, suggestions and solutions that have been proposed throughout this book. This chapter summarises the two key areas of the problem-solving approach that has been proposed.

The Planning Stage This represents the time that you spend planning your answer to an FAE case study. In the examination it will include the reading time that you have at the beginning of each paper. This is likely to be supplemented by additional time that you allocate to the planning of your answer. During the planning stage, you will assimilate and integrate the case material so that you have a full understanding of the issues that must be addressed and how you should approach them. The planning stage is an integral and essential part of attempting each FAE case study.

The Implementation Stage Here you will be using your plan to address each of the issues in a case. Your answer should be written in a professional manner, employing reasoned arguments that relate to the specific information contained in the case. To display competence to the Examiner, you will be expected to show proficiency in respect of fundamental skills, value-adding skills and advisory skills.

Based on the problem-solving approach outlined above, the following is an overall step-by-step guide to completing an FAE case study.

The Planning Stage

1. Establish what your role is (i.e. who are you in the case?).
2. Identify the primary indicators (and the issues to avoid).
3. Read the case in detail and relate all information to the primary indicators.
4. Draft the 'big picture'.

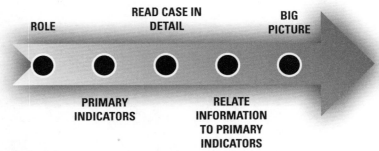

Having completed the planning stage, you are now ready to write your answer.

Implementation Stage

5. Address each primary indicator with points that are specific to the circumstances of the business.
6. Prepare calculations that are essential to address a primary indicator.
7. Achieve depth by the skilful development of your points. Use techniques such as a 'cradle-to-grave' approach, a conflicting-perspectives approach or establishing linkages approach, and integrate the material in the case.
8. Be decisive! Reach a conclusion or make a recommendation, and ensure that this is included in your report.
9. Prepare a relevant executive summary.

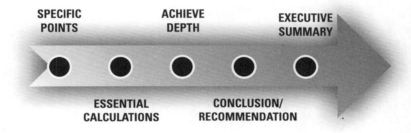

Supplements

Supplement A

FAE CORE COMPREHENSIVE*

Tidy Homes Group

It is now September 2010 and you, Susan Robson, have been in your role as Financial Accountant with the Tidy Homes Group ("THG") for almost one year after recently qualifying as a Chartered Accountant. This is your first role outside of practice and you have fitted in well with the THG finance team, developing good working relationships with everyone. You are excited about the opportunities that lie ahead for you as you feel you are applying and building on your skills and adding value to the Group. Your employment contract is with Tidy Holdings Ltd and you report to the group finance director, Cathy Crawford.

THG is a privately held group of companies owned by a husband and wife team, Mary and Peter Jones. Mary set up the business more than 20 years ago, offering home cleaning services in her local area. In the early days Mary did the cleaning work herself, but as the economy strengthened and demand for personal services such as cleaning rose, Mary expanded her business by taking on staff and offering cleaning services across a larger geographic area. During the economic boom years of the 1990s and early 2000s, as personal incomes rose, the business did very well and continued to grow very rapidly with additional services being added. THG now consists of a holding/management company that looks after all the administrative services for the Group (Tidy Holdings Ltd); Tidy Homes Ltd which provides personal home cleaning services to private individuals; Tidy Offices Ltd which provides contract office and workplace cleaning services to businesses; and Tidy Gardens Ltd which provides gardening services to private individuals and outdoor facilities management services to businesses (see Group and Board Structures in Appendix 1). THG now employs more than 700 people, has a turnover in the region of €/£25 million and operates across all of Ireland.

Over the past few months, as you have been working on the management accounts of the Group, you have noticed that the trading results have been getting consistently poorer. Your worst fears are confirmed when you are requested to attend a meeting with your boss, Cathy Crawford.

---

* Taken from Paper 1 Autumn 2010. Based on the 2009/2010 FAE Competency Statement.

Meeting with Cathy Crawford, THG Group Finance Director

"Susan, as you are aware, I will be out of the office and not contactable for the next two weeks. Unfortunately there is a lot that I need prepared before the next Board meeting. I have agreed with the other members of the Board that, given my upcoming absence, I can bring you into my confidence and get you to start to work on the report that I have to give them in a month's time.

"To bring you up to speed, the Board is becoming increasingly concerned about the trading performance of the Group. As I am sure you have noticed, things are not currently going well and we are facing very difficult trading conditions. The economic downturn over the past couple of years is really beginning to bite, and as a Group we need to make plans and take some drastic action to ensure that we survive the current crisis and are well placed to move forward again when things begin to turn. I had been reviewing the management accounts against our projections for the year and decided that, as we were so far off target, it was time to update our projections for the remainder of the financial year (FY) 2010. Here is a copy of my revised projections that I presented to the Board at last Friday's meeting (Appendix 2).

"The Board discussed the severity of the situation at length and we have formulated a high level plan of action that we feel we may need to implement in the forthcoming financial year. I want you to work on the first draft of the report that I am to present to the Board at the next meeting. I know there is a lot to cover in the next four weeks so please make this your top priority. It obviously goes without saying that you need to keep this to yourself as we don't want to alarm anyone unnecessarily.

"Here is a copy of the Draft Board Minutes from last Friday's meeting (Appendix 3). Everything you need to address in the report should be in there. I have started to make some notes that may be of use to you – just in relation to the management information pack and also the staff efficiency assumptions agreed by the Board; here they are (Appendix 6). I have not yet had time to look at the possible closure of Tidy Gardens in detail. Could you consider all the relevant implications should we decide to proceed with that option? I would appreciate it if you could have your first draft ready for my return and we can work together on it further then.

"If any other significant suggestions or issues occur to you when you are working on the report, please don't hesitate to include them and we can discuss them also when I return."

Students should assume that the figures for tax charges in the Appendices are appropriate for their jurisdiction (i.e. ROI or NI as appropriate).

APPENDIX 1: **GROUP AND BOARD STRUCTURE**

Group Equity Shareholding Structure

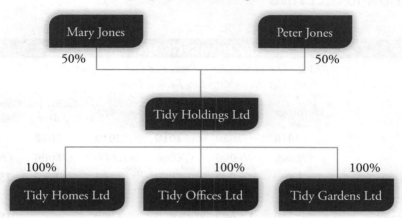

Board of Directors (for Individual Companies and the Group):

- Mary Jones, 50, Managing Director, founder of THG.
- Peter Jones FIPD, 51, HR Director, with THG for 18 years, previously HR Director for the Irish division of a large multinational software company.
- Cathy Crawford FCA, 48, Finance Director, with THG for 15 years, qualified as a CA 23 years ago.
- Noel Campbell, 45, Operations Director, with THG for 10 years.
- Greg Wylie FCA, 67, Non-executive Chairman, former partner with a 'Big 4' accountancy firm.
- Amy McKenna MBA, 58, Non-executive Director, successful, retired businesswoman.
- Patrick McComb, 44, Non-executive Director, currently the Owner and Managing Director of a medium-sized local manufacturing company.

NEDS

The Board meets once a month to review the performance of THG (and each individual company) and develop and implement the strategy of the Group. A comprehensive management information pack is provided to all Board members in advance of the meeting. Detailed minutes and votes on Board decisions are kept. The Board follows best practice corporate governance guidelines.

APPENDIX 2: REVISED FY 2010 PROFIT & LOSS PROJECTIONS FOR YEAR ENDED 31 DECEMBER 2010 – AS PRESENTED AT THE BOARD MEETING

	Holdings	Homes	Offices	Gardens	Consol Adj	Consoli-dated
TIDY HOMES GROUP						
REVISED Full Year 2010 Profit and Loss Projection (July Mgt Accs + Aug–Dec Revised Projections)						
	2010	2010	2010	2010	2010	2010
	€/£000	€/£000	€/£000	€/£000	€/£000	€/£000
Turnover	4,500	6,000	14,000	5,000	(4,500)	**25,000**
Direct wages	0	5,600	10,400	2,900		**18,900**
Direct materials and overheads	0	1,320	3,360	750		**5,430**
Gross Profit	**4,500**	**(920)**	**240**	**1,350**	**(4,500)**	**670**
Costs:						
Management charges	0	1,500	1,500	1,500	(4,500)	**0**
Selling costs	0	700	1,000	200		**1,900**
Executive directors' remuneration	2,500	0	0	0		**2,500**
Non-executive directors' fees	66	0	0	0		**66**
Travel and subsistence	200	0	0	0		**200**
Admin staff costs	640	0	0	0		**640**
Admin overheads	1,000	0	0	0		**1,000**
Total Costs	**4,406**	**2,200**	**2,500**	**1,700**	**(4,500)**	**6,306**
Operating Profit/ (Loss)	**94**	**(3,120)**	**(2,260)**	**(350)**	**0**	**(5,636)**

	Holdings	Homes	Offices	Gardens	Consol Adj	Consoli- dated
	2010	2010	2010	2010	2010	2010
	€/£000	€/£000	€/£000	€/£000	€/£000	€/£000
Taxation						1,500
Profit/(Loss) after Tax						(4,136)
Number of direct staff	0	200	400	100		700
Number of executive directors	4	0	0	0		4
Number of admin staff	20	0	0	0		20

APPENDIX 3: DRAFT BOARD MINUTES

Board Minutes of Tidy Homes Group held on 31 August 2010

Present: MJ Mary Jones
PJ Peter Jones
CC Cathy Crawford
NC Noel Campbell
GW Greg Wylie (Chairman)
AM Amy McKenna
PM Patrick McComb

1. Board Minutes

GW opened the meeting; the draft minutes of the previous Board meeting were read. As no amendments were proposed, a vote was taken with all members agreeing to approve and officially enter the minutes of the previous meeting into the Minute Book.

2. July 2010 Accounts & Management Information

CC presented the Board with the July 2010 management accounts. CC commented that the economic climate has continued to worsen and trading performance has again declined. NC confirmed CC's prognosis of the economic climate and provided the Board with a report outlining the continued decline in the number of contracts held by each division of the Group.

CC feared that, although the Group had taken the current economic crisis into consideration when the initial budgets were produced, the actual decline in the business was happening faster and deeper than had been anticipated in the Group's budget for the FY 2010. CC presented to the Board a revised projection of Group trading performance to the end of the FY.

CC proposed that, given the severity of the current financial crisis, it would be a prudent step to review the management information currently being produced within the Group to see what, if any, improvements could be made to it to help the Board (and management team) manage the Group's current performance and ensure that any potential issues arising would be spotted swiftly. All present agreed that this would be a sensible step and that CC should carry out a review and make any improvement recommendations she felt would be of benefit at the next meeting.

3. Current Economic Climate/Action Plan

On reviewing the revised projections to the end of the FY 2010 (Appendix 2) provided by CC, a detailed discussion followed about how best to protect THG from the worsening economic climate and ensure that the Group was well placed to ride out a further year of economic recession. It was agreed by all that CC should prepare a report for the Board including a first draft of projections for the FY 2011 based on consideration of the following:

- ■ Anticipation of a further 10% reduction in business levels of both Tidy Homes Ltd and Tidy Offices Ltd.
- ■ Possibility of closing Tidy Gardens Ltd (considered to be a non-core business to Group operations).
- ■ Reduction of headcount of direct staff to the levels required to carry out the anticipated level of business. *ie 10% less* .
- ■ Outsourcing the Group's IT function (see point 5. below). *Need more info* .
- ■ Not awarding pay rises in FY 2011.

Following further discussions it was agreed that CC should also include in her report any tax and financial reporting implications arising from the current situation of the business (including any implications if all or any of the above actions are implemented). All agreed that any report should focus on the future and not historical performance. *comparison Tax losses cff ...*

4. Report of Audit Committee

GW reported to the Board that the audit committee (GW, AM and PM) had met with Graham Hunter (Audit Partner) of ABC Auditors during the month to make preparations for the interim audit of THG that has now been scheduled to take place in November 2010. GW told the Board that during the meeting Graham Hunter congratulated CC and said how impressed he had been with the level of information produced by CC and her team and that no other matters of significance were found during the audit process. On behalf of the Board, MJ expressed congratulations to CC and her team for all the hard work and effort that obviously went into running such a smooth finance department. *Good audit info* .

Also, during the pre-interim audit meeting, Graham Hunter had commented that, although the previous year's accounts (FY 2009) had been signed off (in May 2010) with an unqualified audit report and on a going concern basis, this year the auditors would carry out more tests and pay more attention to the preparation of accounts on a going concern basis. Graham Hunter explained that, because of the new going concern guidelines, his firm was unable to give an unqualified audit report to many well established and formerly successful companies. Following a discussion it was agreed by all that, for the next Board meeting, CC should include in her report recommendations as to what evidence THG would need to be able to supply to the auditors to ensure that an unqualified opinion could be given for the FY 2010 audit and highlight any potential difficulties in this regard.

5. Outsource IT Proposal

PJ presented the Board with a proposal from ALL IRELAND IT Ltd in relation to the Group outsourcing its internal IT function to this company. PJ and MJ further explained that ALL IRELAND IT Ltd was a company recently set up by their nephew and that they would like to assist him in getting his business off the ground. MJ continued that if the proposal made financial sense she would like the Board to consider accepting it. All agreed that CC should review the proposal and detail her findings at the next Board meeting.

The meeting was then brought to a close by GW. The next meeting will be in four weeks' time at the end of September 2010.

Related Party

④⁷

APPENDIX 4(A): SUMMARY OF HISTORICAL FINANCIAL STATEMENTS FOR YEAR ENDED 31 DECEMBER

			TIDY HOMES GROUP			

Summary 2009 Management Accounts: Profit and Loss Account
(based on audited figures)

	Holdings	Homes	Offices	Gardens	Consol Adj	Consoli-dated
	2009	2009	2009	2009	2009	2009
	€/£000	€/£000	€/£000	€/£000	€/£000	€/£000
Turnover	4,200	↓ 8,000	↓16,500	↓ 5,000	(4,200)	**29,500**
Direct wages	0	↑ 5,300	↑ 10,200	2,850		**18,350**
Direct materials and overheads	0	1,680	3,795	750		**6,225**
Gross Profit	4,200	1,020	2,505	1,400	(4,200)	4,925
Costs:						
Management Charges	0	1,400	1,400	1,400	(4,200)	**0**
Selling costs	0	↑ 600	↑ 900	200		**1,700**
Executive directors' remuneration	2,200	0	0	0		**2,200**
Non-executive Directors' fees	63	0	0	0		**63**
Travel and subsistence	200	0	0	0		**200**
Admin staff costs	620	0	0	0		**620**
Admin overheads	1,000	0	0	0		**1,000**
Total Costs	4,083	2,000	2,300	1,600	(4,200)	5,783
Operating Profit/ (Loss)	117	(980)	205	(200)	0	(858)

	Holdings	Homes	Offices	Gardens	Consol Adj	Consolidated
	2009	**2009**	**2009**	**2009**	**2009**	**2009**
	€/£000	**€/£000**	**€/£000**	**€/£000**	**€/£000**	**€/£000**
Taxation						283
Loss after Tax						(575)
Number of direct staff	0	200	400	100		**700**
Number of executive directors	4	0	0	0		**4**
Number of admin staff	20	0	0	0		**20**

APPENDIX 4(B): SUMMARY OF HISTORICAL FINANCIAL STATEMENTS FOR YEAR ENDED 31 DECEMBER

TIDY HOMES GROUP

Summary 2008 Profit and Loss Accounts (based on audited figures)

	Holdings	Homes	Offices	Gardens	Consol Adj	Consoli-dated
	2008	2008	2008	2008	2008	2008
	€/£000	€/£000	€/£000	€/£000	€/£000	€/£000
Turnover	4,000	9,000	17,000	6,000	(4,000)	**32,000**
Direct wages	0	5,000	10,000	2,800		**17,800**
Direct materials and overheads	0	1,800	3,740	900		**6,440**
Gross Profit	**4,000**	**2,200**	**3,260**	**2,300**	**(4,000)**	**7,760**
Costs:						
Management charges	0	1,333	1,333	1,334	(4,000)	**0**
Selling costs	0	500	800	200		**1,500**
Executive directors' remuneration	2,000	0	0	0		**2,000**
Non-executive directors' fees	60	0	0	0		**60**
Travel and subsistence	200	0	0	0		**200**
Admin staff costs	600	0	0	0		**600**
Admin overheads	1,000	0	0	0		**1,000**
Total Costs	**3,860**	**1,833**	**2,133**	**1,534**	**(4,000)**	**5,360**
Operating Profit/ (Loss)	**140**	**367**	**1,127**	**766**	**0**	**2,400**

	Holdings	Homes	Offices	Gardens	Consol Adj	Consolidated
	2008	2008	2008	2008	2008	2008
	€/£000	€/£000	€/£000	€/£000	€/£000	€/£000
Taxation						(792)
Profit after Tax						1,608
Number of direct staff	0	200	400	100		700
Number of executive directors	4	0	0	0		4
Number of admin staff	20	0	0	0		20

APPENDIX 5: HISTORICAL AND PROJECTED GROUP BALANCE SHEET

TIDY HOMES GROUP

Consolidated Balance Sheets as at 31 December (based on audited figures)

	2008	2009	2010
	Audited	**Audited**	**Projected**
	€/£000	**€/£000**	**€/£000**
Fixed Assets (Property, Plant and Equipment)	400	425	450
Current Assets:			
Stock	920	1,038	1,386
Trade debtors	2,521	2,789	3,257
Prepayments and accrued income	450	450	450
Director's loan – Peter Jones	500	500	500
Other debtors	0	283	1,600
Bank and cash	8,678	6,888	994
Total Current Assets	13,069	11,948	8,187
Current Liabilities:			
Trade creditors	864	1,006	1,343
Accruals and deferred income	200	200	325
Other creditors	2,205	1,492	1,380
Total Current Liabilities	3,269	2,698	3,048
Net Current Assets	9,800	9,250	5,139
Long-term Creditors and Provisions			
Director's loan – Mary Jones	2,000	2,000	2,000
Other provisions	600	650	700
Total Long-term Creditors	2,600	2,650	2,700
Net Assets	7,600	7,025	2,889
Share Capital and Reserves			
Share capital	100	100	100
Profit and loss account	7,500	6,925	2,789
Total Share Capital and Reserves	7,600	7,025	2,889

APPENDIX 6: NOTES PROVIDED BY CATHY CRAWFORD

Management Information Review

- Current monthly information pack produced (all given to Board):
    - Monthly profit and loss accounts for each company and consolidated.
    - Monthly balance sheets for each company and consolidated.
    - Monthly cashflow statements for each company and consolidated.
    - All the above statements are compared against a budget and the same period last year.

 ■ Is this the most appropriate monthly information?

Efficiency Assumptions

- Assume 240 working days per year.
- Average charge-out rate per direct staff member = €/£200 per day.
- Aim to achieve efficiency (i.e. recovery rate) of at least 90%.

APPENDIX 7: OUTSOURCING GROUP IT FUNCTION PROPOSAL

All Ireland IT Ltd – Summary of Proposal to Tidy Homes Group for Provision of IT Services

- Guaranteed four business-hours response time.
- First response by telephone support.
- Second response by remote VPN access to systems.
- Third response: on-site visit until problem resolved.
- Implement dedicated 10Mbps direct connection.
- Mirroring of all critical servers.
- Annual management charge = €/£75,000.
- Direct connection charge = €/£18,000 p.a.
- Critical server mirroring = €/£25,000 one-off charge.
- Support billed in units of 15 minutes, average cost = €/£150 per hour.
- Minimum monthly support charge is for 60 hours.
- All consumables and equipment at expense of THG.
- Travel and subsistence billed separately.

Current Internal IT Department

- Current team = three full-time staff: Bill, Ben and Bob; total staff costs are approximately €/£150,000 p.a.
- Other IT department costs approximately €/£75,000 p.a.

Discounted cashflow
for both &
compare NPV.

Supplement B

FAE CORE SIMULATIONS*

Simulation 1: Platinum Software Limited Company ("Platinum")

(Suggested Time: 90 Minutes)

You are Martina Mathews. It is June 2010. You qualified as a Chartered Accountant two years ago and have just completed your first year in a large accountancy practice. You are determined to create the right impression with the new partner heading up your section, John Lampard.

John asks you to attend a meeting with David Hughes, Managing Director and 100% owner of the limited company Platinum. You recall reading an article about Platinum in last month's national newspaper (extract from article replicated in Appendix 1). John is impressed that you have heard of Platinum.

After many calls, emails and messages, you finally organise a meeting for the following week with David in Platinum's new offices. Before the meeting, John organises the signing of the engagement letter and the documents for the anti-money laundering identification procedures.

When you and John meet David, he reminds you of a famous football manager: arrogant, determined, focused and only wants to succeed. He has just been nominated for the most important prize in Ireland for computer technology. He is in such a rush he can only spend 10 minutes with both of you and so you do not get a chance to ask any of the questions you had prepared.

David highlights the following background information:
- His main focus is to drive the business forward through new contracts and research. He knows that this research does not qualify for tax credits.
- He wants to launch a new version of the software in the next few months.
- He spends a lot of his time on perfecting his product, as he recognises that errors in software development lead to customer dissatisfaction.
- The software products are easy to use, reliable and cheaper than competitor products.
- The company has just launched a customer support service. It is expected that the support service will account for 40% of total future revenues. The support service fee will be paid at the time of sale and the service will cover a three-year period.
- Customer support is important and will generate valuable revenue streams.
- He plans to develop the company as a world leader over the next three years but feels a lack of funding resources may hinder this strategy.

---

* Taken from Autumn paper 2010. Based on the 2009/2010 FAE Competency Statement.

91

- He expects sales to continue to grow rapidly particularly in the USA, forecasting that 25% of total sales will be from the USA next year.
- He is concerned about the lack of staff with the relevant IT skills in the Irish market and on-going general cost increases. He notes that all staff are on a fixed salary.
- There are no foreign currency bank accounts.
- The company always invoices clients overseas in their local currency.
- There are no bank borrowings or overdraft facility.
- Gross assets before liabilities are currently €/£4 million.
- **(ROI ONLY)** He has checked and Platinum could raise BES funding in 2010 when it receives employment grants from an industrial development agency, as it will have satisfied all the conditions which a company must satisfy. (He is aware that BES funding could impact on future grant aid.)
- **(NI ONLY)** HMRC confirmed in writing two months ago that the company at that point in time was a qualifying company for EIS purposes.
- Platinum recently engaged the services of Eastwood Consulting to undertake an overall review of the business. (Eastwood Consulting is a well-regarded, reputable management consultancy firm.)

David asks for assistance to address:
- Issues arising from the Eastwood Consulting report (see file note, replicated in Appendix 2). David needs guidance with regard to areas covered in the report and the steps involved in the formulation of a strategic plan as he has never been involved in the preparation of one before.
- A review of the tax considerations relating to a potential investment in the company (David's note of his telephone conversation with Leslie Jenkins, a wealthy individual, is replicated in Appendix 3).

He notes that the financing of the company is being separately addressed by the Corporate Finance Team. In addition he emphasises that any tax advice should be limited to the potential investment mentioned above.

After the meeting John requests that you prepare a memo for his (John's) use, addressing the issues about which David has asked for assistance.

APPENDIX 1: EXTRACT FROM CURRENT NATIONAL NEWSPAPER ARTICLE

Platinum Software creates 10 new jobs and more to follow

Platinum Software, 100% owned by David Hughes, has created 10 new jobs with the opening of new offices. The offices which are the first part of a significant investment will house the technology and commercial departments. Platinum is also planning a back office support centre in an overseas location in the next 12 months for the new version of the software.

Platinum was founded in 2007 by Hughes, a computer science graduate with a PhD from one of Ireland's premier universities. Platinum provides customer relationship management software that facilitates automated telephone calls, texts and email messages. It has won significant contracts in Ireland and the UK, where major retailers for large products, like furniture and electrical goods, use the software to contact clients and schedule home deliveries.

Platinum has achieved substantial revenue growth in the last three years; the software is currently challenging the market leader based in the USA. Platinum is launching a new version of the software with the added feature of customer service support and product updates for a period of three years from date of purchase. Currently all software products are sold without any after-sales service support or update feature.

Platinum's new offices were opened by a Government Minister yesterday. An industrial development agency is providing an employment grant next year of €/£1 million to support the new facility. The new jobs are in the area of software engineering, research and development.

APPENDIX 2: FILE NOTE RE: REPORT FROM JASON EASTWOOD CONSULTANTS

The report contains a general review of Platinum's business.

The review excluded research and development as this was already identified as a weakness by the external auditors and various solutions have already been implemented in order to address these weaknesses. However, the report noted that research and development has been dealt with appropriately from both financial reporting and taxation perspectives.

Summary of Issues Raised

- **Sales:** The accounting policy is to recognise revenue in full at the time of sale.
- **Grants:** Need to confirm appropriate treatment of the new employment grant from an industrial development agency.
- **Costs:** Need to control cost base to remain competitive, particularly payroll costs. Overseas salary costs (in some developing countries) are 10% of those in Ireland.
- **Foreign exchange risk:** Need to identify and agree solutions to manage the currency risk as 10% of sales and 9% of product costs are now in US Dollars.
- **Platinum strategic plan:** Strategic goal identified to be a world leader in 2013, in three years' time. No strategic plan currently in place. Recommend that a strategic plan is developed to support this high-level objective.

APPENDIX 3: DAVID HUGHES'S NOTES OF A TELEPHONE CONVERSATION WITH LESLIE JENKINS (A WEALTHY INDIVIDUAL)

■ Cannot believe Leslie Jenkins called me; he is such a high-profile celebrity and he's married to Agnes Collins (who is independently wealthy). He has €/£1 million to invest immediately.

■ It would be really helpful to have a person of his profile as a shareholder in the company.

■ Wish I knew the answers, sounds like a great idea – how can Leslie Jenkins's potential investment in the company be structured in the most tax efficient manner from his perspective?

■ Who can I trust to give me the best independent advice? Must get in touch with a Chartered Accountant.

APPENDIX 4: PLATINUM SOFTWARE – STATEMENT OF COMPREHENSIVE INCOME FOR THE YEAR ENDED 30 JUNE

PLATINUM SOFTWARE

	2010	2009	2008
	€/£000	€/£000	€/£000
Continuing Operations			
Revenues	6,350	2,400	550
Cost of sales	(762)	(288)	(220)
Gross Profit	**5,588**	**2,112**	**330**
Sales and marketing costs	(1,270)	(480)	(28)
Research and development costs	(1,587)	(600)	(137)
Administrative expenses	(762)	(288)	(27)
Amortisation of intangibles	(150)	(150)	(50)
Operating Profit	**1,819**	**594**	**88**

Profit for the year has been arrived at after charging/(crediting)

EXTRACTS FROM THE NOTES TO THE FINANCIAL STATEMENTS

	2010	2009	2008
	€/£000	€/£000	€/£000
Auditor's remuneration	75	25	10
Foreign exchange differences	(175)	50	(50)

The average number of permanent full-time persons employed during the year was 43 (2009:22) and is as follows:

Staff Numbers	2010 Number	2009 Number	2008 Number
Professional services	6	4	3
Sales and marketing	14	6	0
Research and development	16	8	2
General and administration	7	4	0
Total Staff Numbers	**43**	**22**	**5**

Staff Costs	2010 €/£000	2009 €/£000	2008 €/£000
Wages and salaries	2,970	1,184	212
Social insurance costs	356	142	26
Pension costs	297	118	0
Total Staff Costs	**3,623**	**1,444**	**238**

Supplement C

LINKING CASE INFORMATION AND PRIMARY INDICATORS FAE CORE SIMULATIONS*

Simulation 1: Platinum Software Limited Company ("Platinum")

(Suggested Time: 90 Minutes)

You are Martina Mathews. It is June 2010. You qualified as a Chartered Accountant two years ago and have just completed your first year in a large accountancy practice. You are determined to create the right impression with the new partner heading up your section, John Lampard.

John asks you to attend a meeting with David Hughes, Managing Director and 100% owner of the limited company Platinum. You recall reading an article about Platinum in last month's national newspaper (extract from article replicated in Appendix 1). John is impressed that you have heard of Platinum.

After many calls, emails and messages, you finally organises a meeting for the following week with David in Platinum's new offices. Before the meeting, John organises the signing of the engagement letter and the documents for the anti-money laundering identification procedures.

When you and John meet David, he reminds you of a famous football manager, arrogant, determined, focused and only wants to succeed. He has just been nominated for the most important prize in Ireland for computer technology. He is in such a rush he can only spend 10 minutes with both of you and so you do not get a chance to ask any of the questions you had prepared.

David highlights the following background information:
- His main focus is to drive the business forward through new contracts and research. He knows that this research does not qualify for tax credits.
- He wants to launch a new version of the software in the next few months. **(PI 5) – Strategy**
- He spends a lot of his time on perfecting his product, as he recognises that errors in software development lead to customer dissatisfaction. **(PI 5) – Strategy**
- The software products are easy to use, reliable and cheaper than competitor products. **(PI 5) – Strategy**
- The company has just launched a customer support service. It is expected that the support service will account for 40% of total future revenues. The support service fee will be paid at the time of sale and the service will cover a three-year period. **(PI 2) – Accounting policy**

---

* Taken from Autumn paper 2010. Based on the 2009/2010 FAE Competency Statement.

- Customer support is important and will generate valuable revenue streams. **(PI 5) – Strategy**
- He plans to develop the company as a world leader over the next three years but feels a lack of funding resources may hinder this strategy. **(PI 5) – Strategy**
- He expects sales to continue to grow rapidly particularly in the USA, forecasting that 25% of total sales will be from the USA next year. **(PI 4)** and **(PI 5) – Exchange risk and strategy**
- He is concerned about the lack of staff with the relevant IT skills in the Irish market and on-going general cost increases. He notes that all staff are on a fixed salary. **(PI 3) – Cost base** and **(PI 5) – Strategy**
- There are no foreign currency bank accounts. **(PI 4) – Exchange risk**
- The company always invoices clients overseas in their local currency. **(PI 4) – Exchange risk**
- There are no bank borrowings or overdraft facility.
- Gross assets before liabilities are currently €/£4 million.
- **(ROI ONLY)** He has checked and Platinum could raise BES funding in 2010 when it receives employment grants from an industrial development agency, as it will have satisfied all the conditions which a company must satisfy. (He is aware that BES funding could impact on future grant aid.)
- **(NI ONLY)** HMRC confirmed in writing two months ago that the company at that point in time was a qualifying company for EIS purposes.
- Platinum recently engaged the services of Eastwood Consulting to undertake an overall review of the business. (Eastwood Consulting is a well-regarded, reputable management consultancy firm.)

David asks for assistance to address:
- Issues arising from the Eastwood Consulting report (see file note, replicated in Appendix 2). David needs guidance with regard to areas covered in the report and the steps involved in the formulation of a strategic plan as he has never been involved in the preparation of one before.
- A review of the tax considerations relating to a potential investment in the company (David's note of his telephone conversation with Leslie Jenkins, a wealthy individual, is replicated in Appendix 3). **(PI 1) – Taxation**

He notes that the financing of the company is being separately addressed by the Corporate Finance Team. In addition he emphasises that any tax advice should be limited to the potential investment mentioned above.

After the meeting John requests that you prepare a memo, for his (John's) use, addressing the issues about which David has asked for assistance.

APPENDIX 1: EXTRACT FROM CURRENT NATIONAL NEWSPAPER ARTICLE

Platinum Software creates 10 new jobs and more to follow

Platinum Software, 100% owned by David Hughes, has created 10 new jobs with the opening of new offices. The offices which are the first part of a significant investment will house the technology and commercial departments. Platinum is also planning a back office support centre in an overseas location in the next 12 months for the new version of the software.

Platinum was founded in 2007 by Hughes, a computer science graduate with a PhD from one of Ireland's premier universities. Platinum provides customer relationship management software that facilitates automated telephone calls, texts and email messages. It has won significant contracts in Ireland and the UK, where major retailers for large products, like furniture and electrical goods, use the software to contact clients and schedule home deliveries.

Platinum has achieved substantial revenue growth in the last three years; the software is currently challenging the market leader based in the USA. Platinum is launching a new version of the software with the added feature of customer service support and product updates for a period of three years from date of purchase. Currently all software products are sold without any after-sales service support or update feature. **(PI 2) Accounting policy.**

Platinum's new offices were opened by a Government Minister yesterday. An industrial development agency is providing an employment grant next year of €/£1 million to support the new facility. The new jobs are in the area of software engineering, research and development.

Supplement D

SIMULATION 1*

Simulation 1: Amy

(Suggested Time: 65 Minutes)

You are a newly qualified Chartered Accountant, working in a small practice. Your firm has a reputation for providing a certain amount of voluntary work annually and you have been asked to take part in one of these projects.

Amy is a charity, established four years ago, to help families throughout the world affected by natural disasters. Its objectives are to:
- provide funds to people affected by natural disasters to help rebuild their lives;
- provide volunteers to assist in the rebuilding process; and
- provide a rapid response team to assist in the initial aftermath of disasters.

The charity relies principally on donations from the public, organised fundraising events and its charity shop.

You contact the voluntary Chairperson of Amy, Peter Scott, a local doctor. Peter is delighted to accept your help as he badly needs some financial advice after the charity's recent fraud case, which has been all over the newspapers (Appendix 1). He recognises the importance of appropriate controls within the charity and would gladly welcome your advice in this regard. He is also considering two alternative providers of information systems and has asked for your evaluation and recommendation as to which system would be more appropriate. He has provided you with the information he has gathered to date (Appendix 2).

In light of the charity's specific objectives, you have also been asked to identify suitable KPIs that can be presented to the Board at its next meeting.

---

* Taken from Autumn paper 2011. Based on the 2010/2011 FAE Competency Statement.

APPENDIX 1: **NATIONAL NEWSPAPER ARTICLE**

Charity shop manager stole nearly €/£250,000 over three years

Keith Price stole nearly €/£250,000 from the charity, Amy, that employed him to run its shop. The shop was set up three years ago to help raise additional funds for the charity's relief work in areas affected by natural disasters.

Price siphoned off up to €/£2,000 per week over a three-year period, by using blank cheques signed by colleagues that he then paid into his personal bank account.

Price had matrimonial problems, which had led to an increase in living expenses, and he subsequently left his wife for a younger work colleague and splashed out €/£75,000 on a brand new sports car. If anyone questioned his new-found wealth, Price claimed that he had inherited money from a rich aunt. He hid his scam by producing fake invoices.

Peter Scott, the Chairman of Amy, said: "The loss of the money from the shop has slowed down the charity's programme of helping families devastated by natural disasters throughout the world. We are extremely concerned that the publicity surrounding the case will have an adverse impact on future donations and sales in the charity shop. We will address the fraud issues and implement a new management information system to improve controls and procedures and protect the assets of the charity."

Today, Judge Helen Giggs sentenced Price, a father of two, to jail for four years and nine months. Sentencing him, Judge Giggs said: "People trusted you and you betrayed that trust. Stealing from a charity is a despicable crime." The judge also commented that she was shocked at the lack of controls and procedures within the charity, and was concerned that the fraud had not been identified earlier.

APPENDIX 2: COMPARISON OF COSTS AND BENEFITS OF SYSTEMS A AND B

For a New Management Information System

	SYSTEM A	SYSTEM B
	€/£	€/£
Costs		
Hardware (Year 0 Only)	65,000	75,000
Software (Year 0 Only)	95,000	250,000
Annual maintenance fee (none in Year 0)	50,000	10,000
Staff implementation costs (Year 0 only)	45,000	15,000
Benefits		
Annual cost savings (commencing in Year 1)	90,000	115,000
Other benefits (Year 0 only)	15,000	20,000
Other Information		
Rental of existing charity shop	100,000	100,000
Previous system evaluation costs	10,000	10,000
Supplier established	10 years	2 years
Market reputation	Good	Excellent
Hardware and software life	3 years	4 years
Quality of system controls	Basic standard	Very high standard
Location of software provider	Overseas	Local
Discount rate	5%	5%

Supplement E

SAMPLE EXECUTIVE SUMMARY

Simulation 1 – Platinum Software*

1. Accounting Treatment

Revenue Revenue from the provision of a service should be recognised over the period that the service is provided. Therefore, revenue from Platinum's newly-launched customer support service should be recognised on a straight line basis over 3 years.

Employment Grants The grant that Platinum expects to receive next year is a revenue grant. It should be recognised as income in the same period in which the related expenditure is charged to profit or loss. As expenditure to create the new jobs is likely to be incurred next year, the employment grant should also be recorded in profit or loss in that period.

2. Control of Cost Base

Payroll costs represent 80% of Platinum's total costs. Measures to control payroll costs are outlined in the main report:
- consider outsourcing some services to a low cost economy; or
- replace the salary structure with an incentive scheme that links performance with salary.

3. Management of Foreign Exchange Risk

Platinum should consider establishing a US production base, so that an increased amount of costs will be incurred in the same currency as the company's revenues.

4. Strategic Plan

Multi-domestic strategy appears to be optimal for Platinum to operate globally. This will involve product offerings being tailored to market requirements on a region-to-region basis. It is recommended that Platinum undertake a SWOT analysis of the company. An outline analysis is contained in the main report.

5. Tax Efficient Structure for an Investment by Leslie Jenkins

ROI Relief may be available until 2013 under the Business Expansion Scheme. However, the maximum relief is limited to €150,000 per annum. This could be doubled if the investment in Platinum is in the joint names of Leslie and his wife, Agnes. Full details are outlined in the main report.

NI Relief may be available under the Enterprise Investment Scheme (EIS) relief. A number of onerous conditions will have to be complied with by Platinum for three years after Leslie obtains his qualifying EIS shares. Full details are outlined in the main report.

* Taken from Autumn paper 2010. Based on the 2009/2010 FAE Competency Statement.

Solutions to
Practice Exercises

Solutions to Practice Exercises

As outlined in **Chapter 4**, FAE case studies are structured around indicators (directed and, sometimes, self-directed). However, it is important to remember that the structure of your solution **does not** have to mirror that of the suggested solution.* If you group the indicators together differently, this does not matter; the key point is that you recognise the relevant issues and deal with them appropriately in your answer. This point is often misunderstood by FAE candidates and can lead to unnecessary stress and worry in the exam.

Chapter 4

Practice Exercise 4.1 – Identifying Directed Primary Indicators (Supplement B, Platinum Software Case)

Towards the end of page 2 of the Platinum Software case, a review is required of the tax considerations relating to a potential investment in the company. This is the first primary indicator (PI 1).

Page 2 of the case also states that the other issues to be addressed are outlined in Appendix 2. The following primary indicators are identified in Appendix 2:
■ Evaluation of the accounting policy for recognising revenue and for recording the employment grant (PI 2). As both of these issues relate to Financial Accounting and Reporting, they are treated as a single primary indicator;
■ Consideration of the fact that the company must control its cost base (PI 3);
■ The need to identify and agree solutions to manage the company's currency risk (PI 4); and
■ Development of a strategic plan (PI 5).

FAE Core Simulation cases require that approximately three to five indicators be identified. Five indicators have been identified above.

Practice Exercise 4.2 – Identifying Self-directed Indicators

Eight primary indicators have been identified in the Tidy Homes Group case (see **Example 4.1**). On reading the case, in Supplement A, it quickly becomes apparent that the Group is having cash flow problems. Several courses of action are being taken to address these difficulties:
■ review of the management information system;
■ increased monitoring of projections;
■ the possible closure of Tidy Gardens Ltd; and
■ taking steps to ensure that the Group receives a clean audit report.

It will take time, however, for the above actions to improve cash flow. In the meantime, there will have to be a plan for ensuring that the Group does not run out of cash. This may involve disposing of marketable assets, refinancing existing sources of funding or arranging new lines of credit.

Thus, arranging financing options is a critical **self-directed** indicator in the Tidy Homes case.

---

* The solutions outlined here refer specifically to the 2009/2010 or 2010/2011 examinations and so may differ in terms of technical content.

Practice Exercise 4.3 – Identify Issues to Avoid (Tidy Homes Case in Supplement A)

Issue to avoid 1 The following statement appears at the end of note 3 of the Draft Board Minutes in Appendix 3 of the case: "All agreed that any report should focus on the future and not historical performance." This is a clear instruction that all primary indicators should focus on the future. Consequently, analysis of the **group's historical performance is an issue to avoid**, and no time should be spent on addressing this issue.

Issue to avoid 2 In the third paragraph of the meeting with Cathy Crawford (page 2 of the case) it states that: "The Board... have formulated a high level plan of action..." This is a reference to the fact that a strategic plan is in place and, unless you have a good reason for disregarding this statement, the area of strategy should be interpreted as an issue to avoid.

Practice Exercise 4.4 – Identifying Issues to Avoid (Platinum Software Case in Supplement B)

The penultimate paragraph of page 2 of the case states that: "... the financing of the company is being separately addressed by the Corporate Finance Team. In addition... any tax advice should be limited to the potential investment mentioned above." Thus, financing issues are issues to avoid. Apart from a potential investment in Platinum by a private investor, taxation issues are also issues to avoid. Research and development is also identified as an issue to avoid by Appendix 2 of the case.

Chapter 5

Practice Exercise 5.1 – Linking the Case Information and the Primary Indicators

This is provided as a self-assessment example. Review your solution and ensure that you have linked all of the relevant information in the case to one or more primary indicators. To do this you will need to read the suggested solution to the Tidy Homes Group. This will reveal how case information is used to address the primary indicators.

Practice Exercise 5.2 – Issues to Avoid

On the last line of Appendix 1 of the case, it states that: "The Board follows best practice corporate governance guidelines." This is a clear indication that corporate governance issues are **not** to be addressed in this case.

Chapter 6

Practice Exercise 6.1 – Big Picture – Platinum Software

■ Platinum Software is a private company.
■ 100% owned by MD, David Hughes.
■ Company appears to be completely dependent on David Hughes.

- MD's goal is for company to be a world leader in three years' time.
- Major expansion underway in the US.
- Should consider locating part of the business in the US so as to incur costs there, thus reducing the net US Dollar exposure. (**Lecture Note**: this is an example of linking primary indicators, i.e. the company's strategy and its foreign exchange exposure.)
- The security of the company's information and software is a critical issue:
  - protection of its intellectual property; and
  - protection against viruses and hacking.
  (**Lecture Note**: this is an important self-directed indicator. It is based on addressing the IT risk factors that are critical to the company's business.)
- The following are issues to avoid:
  - financing issues; and
  - tax advice, other than that relating to the proposed investment by Leslie Jenkins.

Chapter 8

Practice Exercise 8.1 – Specialist Entity – The Amy Case (This answer is taken from the FAE Board Report 2011)

Primary Indicator 3 The candidate discusses the KPIs relevant to Amy's objectives and activities (as highlighted in the information in the appendices) plus some other basic **relevant** financial KPIs. The candidate must demonstrate the ability to link KPIs to Amy's key objectives and overall performance

The candidate demonstrates competence in Management Accounting (6.7/6.8).

I have identified, based on limited information and knowledge of Amy, the following KPIs relevant to the charity objectives and activities and separately some financial KPIs. These will assist with the Board's regular assessment of how the charity is performing.

The KPIs should be assessed regularly. Depending on the type of KPI, this could be weekly, monthly or annually. Each KPI should be compared to last year, budget/target and other charities in similar organisations (or other suitable benchmark).

Key Performance Indicators based on Charity Objectives and Activities

Demand for services including:
- number of new volunteers;
- number of volunteers leaving the charity;
- response time from disaster occurring to rapid response team in place;
- number of locations where assistance is being provided;
- number of rapid response teams in place;
- number of re-building teams in place;
- number of charity events organised;
- number of volunteers undergoing training;
- number of volunteers not yet in disaster location;
- number of articles to raise awareness about the charity; and
- number of complaints received by countries in which charity operates.

Key Performance Indicators based on Charity Finances

- amount of donations;
- number of donations;
- analysis of donor attrition;
- fundraising by type of charity campaign;
- number of donors making regular donations via standing order/direct debit;
- shop revenues and costs;
- level of government funding;
- expenditure by type of activity highlighted above; and
- administration costs – compared to last year or as a percentage of donations received.

The development of these KPIs should form part of the new management information system and be capable of being generated automatically.

Examiner Comment – Indicator 3 The KPIs identified needed to specifically relate to a charity and the objectives as provided in the case. Given the circumstances of the case, the most important KPIs needed to monitor the impact of the adverse publicity on Amy. In this context, the measuring of donation levels was considered very important.

Candidates had to identify KPIs clearly and in a manner that the reader could understand how the item was to be measured and reported. For example, a KPI simply referring to donations was not sufficient. The candidate needed to be more specific: the number of new donations, level of cancellations of regular donations (e.g. those made by direct debits), amount of donations on a weekly/monthly basis, etc.

Chapter 10

Practice Exercise 10.1 – Possible Closure of Tidy Gardens

The forecast Profit and Loss Projection for Tidy Gardens is shown in Appendix 2 of the case. Tidy Gardens has forecast costs amounting to €1.7 million, of which €1.5 million relates to management charges.

This is the item which stands out in Appendix 2, both because of its size, and also the fact that it arises from a mandatory allocation which results in management charges being allocated to each of the three divisions on an equal basis. This fails to take account of the turnover or staff levels in the divisions.

If the management charges are distributed on a more equitable basis such as turnover, it turns out that Tidy Gardens is the best-performing division. Therefore its closure is not warranted, and Tidy Gardens should continue in operation.

Chapter 11

Practice Exercise 11.1 – Outsourcing Proposal

Outsourcing has significant consequences for the **division that has been manufacturing the component**. Employees in that division may lose their livelihoods, which gives rise to moral and ethical issues. Perhaps, however, there will be opportunities for redeployment to reduce the incidence of redundancies. There will also be a loss of skills, many of which will have been nurtured in the company over a significant time period.

Outsourcing also has implications for the **division that uses the component**. Quality control issues may arise, as the external supplier may fail to meet the company's technical specifications. Also, the external supplier may be servicing the needs of many other customers. This could result in a poorer than expected level of service and there may be delays in the delivery of the outsourced component. The bottom line is that outsourcing will result in a loss of control over the supply of the component.

There may also be implications for the company's **storage and distribution** systems. It may be necessary to carry higher inventories of finished goods, as a contingency against a possible failure by the external supplier to deliver the component on schedule.

From the **overall perspective of the company**, outsourcing will reduce overhead costs and allow more focus on the company's core activities. The closure of the manufacturing division will give rise to significant legal and human resource issues. It will be critical that efficient channels of communication are established with the outsourcing provider and that the provider is monitored as to its financial solvency. It is also vital that a company's goals and strategy are aligned with the objectives of outsourcing.

Analysis The above solution evaluates outsourcing on a 'cradle-to-grave' basis. The implications are considered sequentially for the various stages of the company's operations.

Practice Exercise 11.2 – Proposed Takeover

Proposed Takeover Clearly, the chief executive is in favour of the takeover as he stands to benefit significantly from the deal. From the shareholders' perspective, however, the offer price must be considered in the context of the value of the company's shares. A number of valuation techniques can be employed for this purpose.

The takeover also has implications for the company's workforce, whose employment may not be guaranteed by the new owners. A redundancy package will have to be provided for those employees whose contracts will be terminated. Suppliers may also be at risk, as the new owners may decide to source their supplies elsewhere. Rhyme's customers may also be affected as the new owners may decide to discontinue the supply of certain products.

In the event that the bid is **not** completed, this may have implications for staff morale and for the continuation of the chief executive in his current position.

Profit Maximisation Strategy The proposed profit maximisation strategy may increase the likelihood of the takeover being completed. This depends, however, on the measures being accepted by the company's auditors. Also, changes in accounting policy must be clearly signalled in the financial statements, thus identifying one of the reasons why profit is higher. Further evidence of the strategy may also be unearthed by the bidder at the due diligence stage of the takeover, potentially endangering the completion of the deal.

From the shareholders' perspective, the profit maximisation strategy has other potential disadvantages:
■ a higher tax charge;
■ higher management remuneration (if bonuses are based on profits); and
■ it may be necessary to repeat this profit performance in the next period if the company is still being showcased.

Analysis The solution examines the consequences of the takeover from the perspective of Rhyme Limited's shareholders, its employees and also the company's suppliers.

The implications of the chief executive's profit maximisation strategy are then considered from the perspective of the shareholders, the company's auditors and the party bidding for the company's shares.

The solution to **Practice Exercise 11.2** illustrates how an issue can be explored by considering the conflicting interests and perspective of different stakeholders in Rhyme Limited.

Practice Exercise 11.3 – Establishing Links

Morse Limited has an imbalance in its corporate governance structure. The Board currently comprises skilled craftsmen whose primary focus is on the quality of the company's fireplaces. As a consequence, Morse Limited has made no effort to research changing consumer preferences. Perhaps customers are now more concerned about fashion and price than about ensuring that they get a fireplace which is of top-notch quality.

It is vital that Morse Limited's corporate governance structure be overhauled. The company should appoint Board members who have financial and marketing expertise. This will facilitate Morse's development of a business strategy that will enable them to compete more effectively in the changing fireplace market.

Analysis It is clear that Morse Limited has serious flaws in its corporate governance structure. This has resulted in a business strategy that focuses exclusively on quality while completely ignoring issues of style and pricing. The inevitable consequence has been a decline in the company's sales.

This solution has established a link between Morse's corporate governance structure and its business strategy. This, in turn, identifies a further linkage between the company's strategy and its sales figures. Thus, an overall link has been established between three business disciplines: corporate governance, business strategy and marketing.

Chapter 12

Practice Exercise 12.1 – Accounting Policy Choice

IAS 40 permits an entity to choose either a cost model or a valuation model for investment property. Whichever model is chosen will apply to all of an entity's investment properties.

If Jupiter opts for the **cost model**, its investment property will be accounted for under the rules of IAS 16 *Property, Plant and Equipment*. The buildings' portion of the property would therefore be subject to annual depreciation over its estimated useful life.

Should Jupiter opt for the **fair value model**, the investment property will be accounted for under the rules of IAS 40 *Investment Property*. Periodic depreciation would not be charged, and any changes in value of the property would be recorded in profit or loss. Any gain on the property would be subject to capital gains tax, but this is not levied until the asset is sold. Therefore, the choice of policy, whether cost or fair value, will have no effect on the company's tax liability.

Use of the fair value model could result in significant fluctuations in Jupiter's annual profit. Management bonuses, which are currently linked to performance, would then also be affected by property price movements. As these are outside of management's control, a fall in property prices could adversely affect management morale and incentive levels.

Recommendation Jupiter operates a management bonus scheme, which is based on the company's annual profit. It is recommended that Jupiter use the cost model for investment property as permitted by IAS 40. This will avoid managerial bonuses being affected by property price movements over which management has no control.

Alternatively, the bonus schemes should be amended to exclude the effect of any valuation adjustments relating to investment property. In this event, the choice between fair value and cost models will have no significant implications, and Jupiter can opt for either policy.

Analysis This answer has employed what is broadly a 'cradle-to-grave' approach. First, it outlines the rules pertaining to accounting policy choice. It relates the choice to the company's circumstances, provides a recommendation, and outlines the implications as follows:
■ authoritative guidance is provided by reference to IAS 40;
■ the alternatives (fair value or cost) are evaluated in the context of the specific circumstances of the company;
■ a recommendation is provided; and
■ the implications of that recommendation are outlined.